S.M.A.R.T TIPS
FOR SUCCESS

Pastor Fisayo KETIKU.

S.M.A.R.T TIPS FOR SUCCESS

☆ SOURCE ☆ MIND ☆ ASSOCIATIONS ☆ RESOURCES ☆ TIME

Become the best version of you

See you at the top!

21/11/13.

Dr. Henry Akintunde

AuthorHouse™
1663 Liberty Drive
Bloomington, IN 47403
www.authorhouse.com
Phone: 1-800-839-8640

© 2013 by Dr. Henry Akintunde. All rights reserved.

No part of this book may be reproduced, stored in a retrieval system, or transmitted by any means without the written permission of the author.

Published by AuthorHouse   04/04/2013

ISBN: 978-1-4817-8742-0 (sc)
ISBN: 978-1-4817-8743-7 (hc)
ISBN: 978-1-4817-8744-4 (e)

Any people depicted in stock imagery provided by Thinkstock are models, and such images are being used for illustrative purposes only.
Certain stock imagery © Thinkstock.

This book is printed on acid-free paper.

Because of the dynamic nature of the Internet, any web addresses or links contained in this book may have changed since publication and may no longer be valid. The views expressed in this work are solely those of the author and do not necessarily reflect the views of the publisher, and the publisher hereby disclaims any responsibility for them.

CONTENTS

ACKNOWLEDGEMENTS ix
INTRODUCTION xi

CHAPTER 1 YOUR MOST EXPANDABLE ASSET: THE MIND 1
- o Understanding the Human Mind 2
- o The Power of an Idea 14
- o The Process of an Idea 21

CHAPTER 2 YOUR MOST INVALUABLE ASSET: PEOPLE 27
- o Beyond Teamwork—Community 29
- o The Power of Community 31
- o Principles for successful relationships 35

CHAPTER 3 YOUR MOST DEPLOYABLE ASSET: MONEY 41
- o Understanding the nature of Money 44
- o How to manage and increase your cash flow 46
- o A word on Student Loans 59
- o A guide on how to become debt free 60

CHAPTER 4 YOUR MOST INFLEXIBLE ASSET: TIME 65
- o Understanding the Concept of Time 66
- o The Importance of Time 67
- o Principles for Managing Time 70

- o Time and Opportunity 76
- o A code not de-coded on time 79
- o No candy for alien 82

CHAPTER 5 YOUR MOST DEPENDABLE ASSET: GOD 91
- o Accident or deliberate design? 91
- o The Importance of Source 94
- o The God-factor and the Mind 100
- o The God-factor and People 102
- o The God-factor and Money 103
- o The God-factor and Time 105

CONCLUSION 107
NOTES 109

This book is dedicated to

All the teachers I have had in my life till date
You challenge me
You inspire me
You expand me
You bring out the best in me
You are my most invaluable Asset.

ACKNOWLEDGEMENTS

Thank you to:

My wife Jumoke for encouraging me to complete this book;

JD Modede for your insights on the Power of Community;

Peter Beckley for proof-reading the manuscript.

INTRODUCTION

I first heard the phrase 'best things in life are free' from one of the Professors of Paediatrics in the Medical School where I received my Medical training. Whilst discussing the subject of healthy living, he would often argue that the most important things needed for good health are free. Some of the examples he gave were the air we breathe, water, fruits, vegetables and nuts. He would also argue that the more expensive a commodity is, the higher the likelihood that it is a luxury, not a necessity. As I examined his claim over the years, even in the light of new knowledge, I have found that he was very right.

This principle is not limited to the things we consume only; it applies to all of life. Smiles, happiness, love, friendship, elation, kind words, just to mention a few, are some of the best things that make the world go round. Yet, they cost nothing.

INTRODUCTION

From reading the stories of several successful people and my personal observations over the years, I have come to a conclusion that regarding becoming successful in life; indeed the best things in life are free. Everyone is born with the resources for achieving greatness in them. These resources are in-built in every person as part of design and do not cost a dime. Over time, a person either discovers these resources and puts them to use to achieve success or fails to appreciate the value of these resources to his/her own peril. As the great thinker Henry David Thoreau points out, "Men are born to succeed, not to fail."

Over the years, Public policy experts and sociologists have stressed the effect of external factors, particularly in early life in determining whether or not a person succeeds in later life. Notably, poverty and the cultural environment have been reported by many studies as being significant factors that determine a person's adulthood.

In 2006, Jo Blanden and Steve Gibbons published a study titled 'The Persistence of poverty across generations.' This study examined the magnitude of the link between poverty in childhood and adulthood poverty. It used data from two sets of cohorts; the National Child Development Study (all children born in one week in Britain in 1958) and the British Cohort Study (all children born in one week in 1970). The study examined data of the members of these cohorts in their teens, 1970 and 1980 for the 1958 and 1970 cohorts respectively. The findings of the study revealed that for those who were teenagers in 1970, the chances of remaining poor in the thirties if they were poor as teenagers doubled that of their peers. Also, for those that were teenagers in 1980, the chance of remaining poor in their thirties if they were poor as teenagers was four times that of their peers.

Clearly, the scientific evidence regarding how external factors influence success cannot be ignored and that is not my intention in this book. My position is simple; these findings only tell part of the story, probably the less important part. A closer look at history reveals many people who achieved great success in spite of their difficult backgrounds or low level of formal education. It also reveals people who despite being born into rich and successful families ended up not achieving success in life. Great names like Benjamin Franklin, John D. Rockefeller, Frederick Douglass and Thomas Edison are just a few examples of people who remind us that success in life is not determined by which family a person is born into, or how much education a person acquires. Their lives constantly remind us that the difference is in how much a person utilises his freely given inner resources.

INTRODUCTION

So, the question is what are the resources that make for success? From my personal study of principles of success and reading life stories of successful people, I have come to conclude that successful people differ from unsuccessful people in how they manage and multiply these five life assets, which every person freely possesses:

- A person's most expandable asset is the MIND.
- A person's most invaluable asset is PEOPLE.
- A person's most inflexible asset is TIME.
- A person's most deployable asset is MONEY.
- A person's most dependable asset is GOD.

These five assets are what I summed up into the acronym S.M.A.R.T.

S= Source (God)

M= Mind

A= Associations (People)

R= Resources (Money)

T= Time

Whether a person succeeds or not is dependent on how he/she uses and multiplies these 5 assets: Mind, people, time, money and God. If you have been looking for success in places where it does not exist, my advice to you is look no further than within yourself. What you seek is already in you. In the words of Russel H. Conwell,

> *"Many of us spend our lives searching for success when it is usually so close that we can reach out and touch it."*

In the succeeding chapters, these life assets and their value to achieving success are discussed in detail. This book has been grouped into 5 chapters, one chapter for each of the life assets. Although, each chapter connects with other chapters of the book, every chapter is complete on its own and has its unique message. So you can read this book in any order you want—from the front to the back page if you prefer or starting with the part that interests you the most. In the first chapter, I start with exploring your most expandable asset—The Mind.

CHAPTER 1

YOUR MOST EXPANDABLE ASSET: THE MIND

The Human mind is the most elastic substance on earth. There is no limit to how much it can be stretched. It is the unseen, yet one of the most powerful aspects of the human being. Every field of human existence today is a product of how well the human mind has been developed. With the human mind, we have the ability to learn, unlearn and relearn. Everyone was born with a capacity to create the world that they want. That capacity is innate in the Mind. Some people discover this truth, put their mind to work and the result is that they create the life they desire. Unfortunately, many others put a limitation on what they can do, and the result is a life they do not either desire or deserve.

Understanding the Human Mind

Lots of research has been undertaken over time to understand the human mind and how it works. From many of these published works, we know that the human mind is complex and that there are levels of functioning of the human mind. A lot has been published about the anatomy, physiology and psychology of the human mind. I do not intend to repeat all these in one book. As a matter of fact, it's impossible to do so.

My intention however is to focus on the workings of the mind that makes for success in life. Personally, I feel the understanding of this aspect of the functioning of the human mind is life-changing. I was fortunate to gain this understanding as a young Christian from reading the bible. Biblical statements like 'As a man thinks, so is he' and 'Guard your heart with all diligence, for out of it flow the issues of life' revealed to me the power of a person's thought. It helped me understand that a man's life literally moves in the direction of his strongest thought. As a result, it's important that you choose carefully what you think on. This has been my life principle since I was a teen. It does not matter how things may appear in reality, I always make the conscious choice of thinking only positive thoughts. The outcome is that I constantly get results that align with my thoughts.

Although, I had understood and applied this principle for nearly two decades, it was not until two years ago that I came to understand the science behind it. I am grateful to Christian Simpson, Professional Coach and member of board of the John Maxwell Team for introducing me to this concept. The experience of understanding the science behind this principle was as equally satisfying as the very first time I discovered this truth. I now want to share this understanding with you.

Much of the understanding of the role of the mind in human performance today is centred on the work of Dr. Thurman Fleet. Dr Fleet was a Chiropractor in the San Antonio area of Texas in the 1930s. In the early years of his practice, Dr Fleet followed closely the scientific theories and methods that he had learnt during his training to become a Chiropractor. After a while however, he became quite concerned by the unevenness of the clinical results of his practice among his patients. As a result of this concern, Dr Fleet began undertaking informal research in his practice by keeping detailed records of the outcomes of his clients.

The findings of this research ultimately led him to formulate the principles that would later be known as the Concept Therapy. This theory essentially teaches that each individual is a triune being consisting of a body, mind and soul. Any of these parts can become out of tune with the other, with the resultant effect being illness. So, he devised a strategy which enabled him to start to treat his patients holistically, a therapy which incorporated care for their body, mind and soul. He opined that a clear understanding of how the different components of Man work would enable physicians identify the origin of a person's illness i.e. whether it is a physical cause or caused by the mind or some spiritual act. He argued that this understanding in turn will enable the physician develop a mental picture of what (s)he desires to see happen under treatment. If the Physician is in turn effectively able to communicate this mental picture to the patient, provided the patient believes in what the physician is trying to achieve, the patient will see the same picture in his/her mind. This mental picture in the patient now repeatedly impressed upon the patient's subconscious turns the innate power in the patient's subconscious loose. That power will ultimately reproduce in the patient's body exactly that which was mentally pictured. The result of the application of this principle by Dr Thurman was a significant improvement in the outcomes of his patients over several years.

Since that time till now, the principle enunciated in Concept Therapy has been incorporated into several aspects of human practice, not in any way limited to the Medical Field. The same principle is now widely used in what is now commonly known as Cognitive Behavioural Therapy.

To help his patients achieve greater clarity of what he was seeking to achieve with their health, Dr Fleet developed a graphic concept now popularly known as the 'Stick Person'. The Stick Person graphic was designed to provide a visual representation of how that which is unseen; the human mind works. This is because as humans, we think in pictures. If there is no clear picture in a person's mind to work with, then there is confusion and the end result is a failure to achieve the desired outcome.

In the next couple of paragraphs, I illustrate perhaps the most important understanding to improving performance and creating success through harnessing the incredible potential of the mind using the stick person graphic. Notice the two circles below, the upper and bigger circle denotes the mind, the smaller one denotes the body. The significant difference in the size of both circles is not an error on my part, it is deliberate. As a matter of fact, the sizes understate the difference between the potential of the human mind and that of the body.

Think about this for a minute, in what way does a person differ from a dog or any other animal you may want to compare a person with? I suspect you have several answers, however all your answers are likely to be traceable to the activity of the human mind. Essentially, as far as the body is concerned nearly every organ or structure you find in the human body can also be found in these other animals. Unfortunately, many of us focus too much on that seen part of us that is limited to our five senses. We fail to realise that our greatest potential lies in the unseen part of us, the mind and not our physical body. In actual fact, the mind controls the activity of the body.

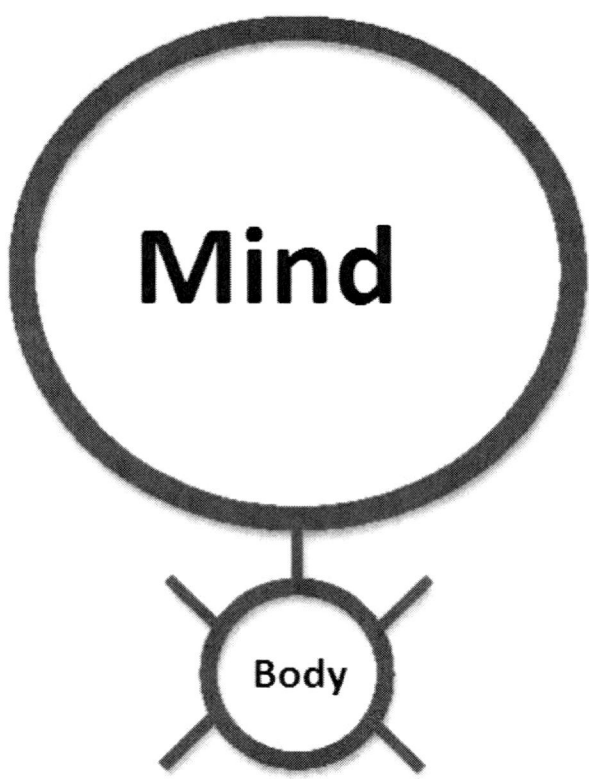

Stickman Image: Courtesy, Dr Thurman Fleet

The mind can be broadly divided into two parts, the conscious mind and the unconscious mind. The conscious mind is your seat of consciousness. In here also lie your will, intellect and conscious reasoning. This is the part of your mind where you exercise the power of choice. With the conscious mind, you can decide to accept or reject an idea. It is also the part of your mind where your five senses feed into. So all the information you get from your environment through seeing, hearing, feeling and smell feedback to this part of the mind where it is interpreted and given meaning. If a person decides to change the direction in which their life is heading, to arrive at that decision, such a person would have actively engaged the conscious part of their mind. So the conscious mind is indeed a very powerful and important part of the human mind.

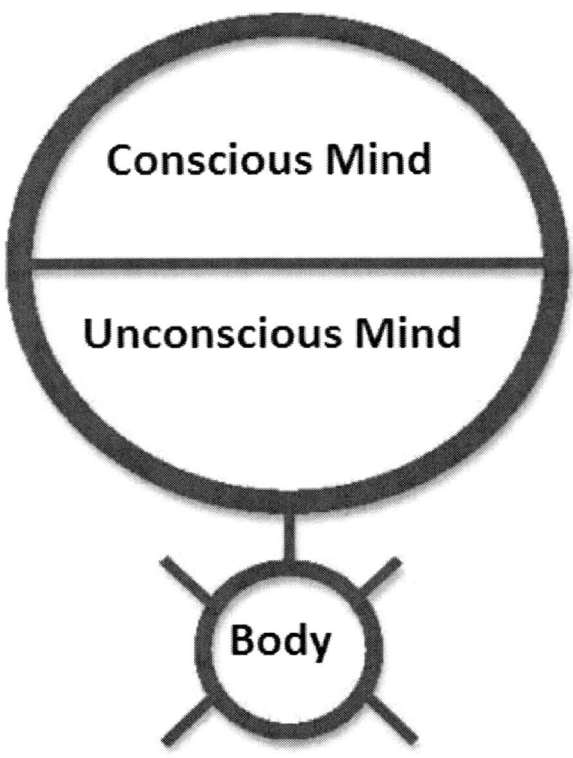

Stickman Image: Courtesy, Dr Thurman Fleet

Although the Conscious mind is where reasoning is done and actions decided upon, it is not the part of the mind responsible for effecting the desired action. That responsibility lies with the second part of the mind called the unconscious mind. The unconscious mind is that part of your mind with which you react to life. All of your memories, pleasant and unpleasant, belief systems and emotions reside in this part of your mind. It is also where your sense of self esteem lies. Whilst the conscious mind is very powerful, it is not as powerful as the unconscious mind. Right now as you read this book, several billions of processes are running in your mind, utilising trillions of cells all at the same time. For example, you are breathing in oxygen, breathing out carbon-dioxide, your heart is pumping blood, your last meal is being digested right now and your kidneys are filtering waste out of your body; all happening simultaneously as you try to make sense of what you are reading. All of these activities and processes are controlled by the unconscious mind. None of them requires your consciousness to happen.

Dr Gary Schmid, an independent Mind-Body Expert in Switzerland believes that in actual fact, only about 0.01% of the activities that take place in a person's mind at any time comes to his/her consciousness. In the words of Dr Schmid, "It is as if roughly 10,000 cinema films are actually going on in the brain all at once, while we are only consciously aware of one of them, indeed, a very particular one transmitted through the sensory channels (sight, smell, sound, taste, touch and balance)"

Bruce Lipton, an internationally recognised development biologist and bestselling author of 'The Biology of Belief' estimates that the processing power of the conscious mind is around 2,000 bits per second. This is pretty impressive statistic. Now consider the processing power of the unconscious mind which is estimated as four billion bits per second. Now that's astonishing.

As astonishing as the working of the unconscious mind is, it can be limited in its operation by what is impressed upon it by the conscious mind. This knowledge is very crucial to Success. **The unconscious mind cannot reject any idea impressed upon it by the conscious mind.** It can only accept an idea; its ability is only deductive in nature. Remember, the decision to accept or reject an idea happens in the conscious mind. Once an idea has been accepted at this level, it is passed on to the unconscious mind, where it is automatically accepted. The thoughts impressed upon the unconscious mind in turn generate feelings. These feelings are expressed by the body under the control of the unconscious mind. The outcome of this process is the results you get in life. This essentially means that the results that you have achieved till today is a function of the thoughts you have impressed on your mind till date. Your thoughts help to release your potential. Remember that the unconscious mind is unlimited. It has infinite potential. As you increase your awareness of your potential, you increase the results you get in your life. This is why I affirm that a person's mind is his/her most expandable asset.

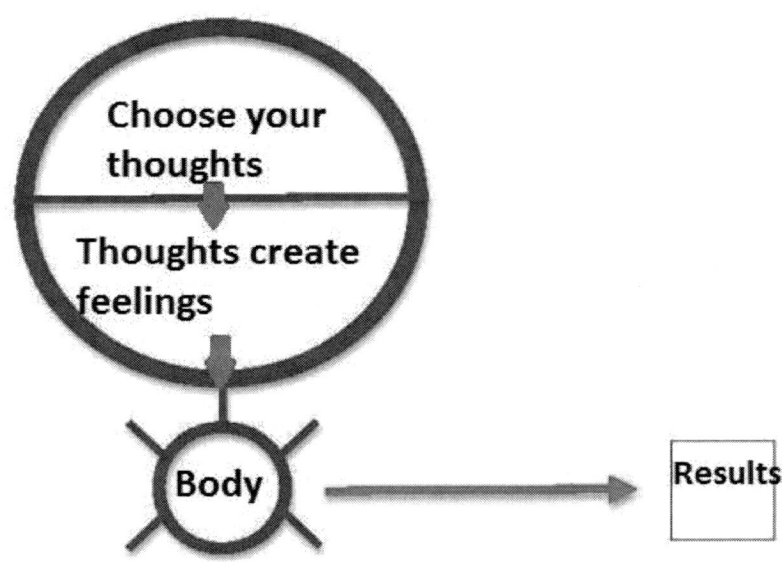

Stickman Image: Courtesy, Dr Thurman Fleet

Any idea that is repeatedly impressed upon the unconscious mind becomes ingrained in it. It moves from the level of a conscious decision to an unconscious habit. Think about driving for a second. Try and recall the very first time you tried to drive a car. I bet you consciously made every movement required to drive the car. If you have been driving for at least a few years now, think about your driving today. I suspect that not only have you become more confident in driving a car, but many of the movements now come automatically to you. Guess what has happened to you? Your driving is now under the control of your unconscious mind because you have repeatedly impressed the same ideas on it.

You are no longer taking an action but a re-action (an action that has been previously taken).

This knowledge again underscores the importance of carefully choosing your thoughts and filtering what you choose to believe. In the words of the wisest man who ever lived, 'As a man thinks in his heart, so is he'. Your life will head in the direction of your strongest thoughts; those that you choose to believe and accept. If you think and believe that there is more to your life than meets the eye; if you believe and accept that you can achieve success no matter the odds against you, then nothing can truly stop you. So here is my question to you, what is your dominant thought?

> *"Whatever you vividly imagine, ardently desire, sincerely believe, and enthusiastically act upon . . . must inevitably come to pass!"* **Paul J. Meyer**

Here is a hypothetical example to reinforce the core of the message so far. A 35 year old married gentleman with two kids (aged five and two), who works as a shop assistant wakes up in the morning, looking forward to the day. He listens to the news before leaving for work and hears that the country is on the verge of experiencing a triple dip recession. He goes to work and during his lunch break, he has a chat with some of his work colleagues who say to him that they have heard some information that the company will be down-sizing within the coming weeks. He closes work and leaves for home at the end of the day, thinking about all he's taken in. All he can think of is him losing his job and fearing the worst for his family, especially his young kids. Out of the blues or so he thinks, he starts to become very anxious, feeling his heart racing and sweaty. He wonders where these symptoms have come from. The symptoms eventually settle after about half an hour.

In the weeks that follow, he continues to ponder on the previous discussion with his work colleagues, with the media constantly reinforcing the same theme. He finds that he continues to experience anxiety symptoms every day, sometimes two to three times a day. After 4 weeks of experiencing these symptoms, he decides to see his Family doctor who diagnoses him with Anxiety Disorder. He wonders why and how this has happened to him. He may not know why, but you my dear reader now know why and how. He got some information and interpreted it as negative information. Unfortunately, he chose to believe what he heard. The idea in turn was accepted by his unconscious mind where a negative feeling was generated. This feeling then manifests in his body as symptoms of anxiety. Over the weeks, the cycle is repeated several times; ultimately his unconscious mind becomes trained to repeat these feelings even when there is no obvious trigger. The result for him is now Anxiety disorder.

Although this is just an example, it is not far from the reality many people experience daily, particularly at these 'difficult economic times'. The only problem here is that many people do not trace the source of their problem to a thought they chose to accept. In the example given, the person in question could have chosen to believe that a difficult economy does not necessarily mean he would lose his job. Even in the event that he loses his job, he could choose to believe that he would find another job or even start his own business. This thought would have generated a whole different feeling which would have resulted in an entirely different outcome. You need to realise that you always have the power to choose what you believe. Your belief will in turn determine your results.

The Power of an Idea

The World as it is today is literarily the product of the many ideas of several people past and present. Can you imagine being born two hundred years ago? You would have been living at a time when there were no cars, no underground trains, no aeroplanes, no internet, no mobile phones and certainly no I-Pads. All the things you may feel are every day necessities today were essentially non-existent two hundred years ago. We owe their existence today to the many people who over the years conceived the ideas for these products and implemented their ideas.

Ideas are not limited to the technological world, every area of human existence continues to be defined and re-defined by human ideas. I recall an article in my undergraduate set's graduation yearbook by one of the Deans in our College of Medicine. In that article, he stressed the need for us as new doctors to be committed to continuing professional development, stating that at least half of the things we learnt in Medical School would be obsolete in five years. Today, I can say that he was very right. Not only have more than half the knowledge I gained as a Medical student become obsolete, the entire way in which the profession of Medicine is practised has changed significantly and continues to change. It's all the product of ideas of people; ideas of how things can be done in a new and better way.

In the same line of thought, the world tomorrow will be defined by the ideas of the many, both in the present and in the future. Our world will continue to be shaped and re-shaped by ideas. In my considered opinion, an idea is one of the greatest products of the human mind. It is a very potent resource for achieving success. In fact, Success in life starts with an idea. Henry Ward Beecher once said, "The ability to convert ideas to things is the secret of outward success."

Right now, you are reading a copy of this book, first and foremost because I had an idea to write this book. If I had not conceived the idea to write this book, it would simply not exist. Similarly everything you do, have and become in life, starts with an idea. The idea may not always originate from you, but you choose whether or not to run with it. I believe strongly that anyone can improve the quality of their life by improving the quality of their ideas. You are just one good idea away from the change you seek.

Allow me to share some interesting things that I have discovered about the power of ideas.

A. Ideas are real

Do you often hear people say they are working on transforming their ideas to reality? By implication, they do not believe that their ideas are real. This is an error of assumption. An idea though unseen is as real as its eventual physical manifestation; it's just in a different state or form. Thanks to science, we now understand the water cycle very clearly. We know that water in its liquid form translates into a gaseous form through the process of evaporation. The gaseous form in turn collects as the cloud and rains in the liquid form back to earth, eventually completing the cycle. No one sees the gaseous form of water; however, this does not change the fact that it is real. So also is an idea, although not seen, it is very real. It is so real that the physical form of it takes the exact nature of the idea as conceived. An idea is just as the architectural design of a house; it provides the blueprint for the final physical product.

By extension, because an idea is real, it cannot be destroyed. In the days before I came to appreciate the power of an idea, there were several times that I had ideas of things I could do that I ignored. I often ended up buying into other people's suggestion that it could not be done or that the timing was not right. Guess what? Almost always, I would later find someone unknown to me implementing the very same idea that I failed to implement on the ground of excuses. It eventually became clear to me that those ideas never died, they only found other outlets for expression.

B. All Ideas are relative

There is no such thing as a big idea, in the same way as there is no such thing as a small idea. Every idea is either seen as small or big from the point of view of the person who conceives the idea. It is all about perception. Again, I remind you that your mind is your most expandable asset. If you can conceive it, you have the capacity to achieve it.

Most people judge the size of their idea by the things they know about themselves so far. In other words, an idea is considered small by a person if that person has done something bigger than the idea previously. Conversely, an idea is seen as big if the same person has not done anything near the size of the idea previously. The mistake in all of these is that these people judge their potential by what they already know about themselves. By the basic definition of the term 'Potential', this is an error. A person's potential is that which a person can do or become but hasn't done or become. So what you know about yourself to date is not your potential but your awareness of your potential so far. There is a lot more where that came from.

C. There's always a strategy for an Idea

Often a lot of people get stuck in finding a way for their ideas to be transformed to its physical manifestation. This is the phase where a lot of people give up. Many try different strategies and do not succeed. Unfortunately as a result, some conclude that there is no way the particular idea can be achieved. The truth however is, it does not matter how many ways you may have tried and failed, there is still a way that you can try and succeed. All you need to do is find it. Let the famous saying of Thomas Edison be your inspiration,

"I have not failed 10,000 times. I have not failed once. I have succeeded in proving that those 10,000 ways will not work. When I have eliminated the ways that will not work, I will find the way that will work."

D. Ideas take time to grow

Ideas are like seeds, they take time to grow. Every idea that you will ever have will take time to mature and manifest. The early phase of implementing an idea can be the most discouraging. It's the phase where the most effort is required, yet the least rewarding phase. In fact many times, at this phase it often appears as if nothing is happening. The truth however is that it only seems like nothing is happening, a lot is truly happening. Let's take human pregnancy for example, very few people unless told, will know that a woman is pregnant within her first two months of pregnancy. This is because the effect of the pregnancy is not visible as yet. However, this same period is perhaps the most crucial phase of pregnancy. All the essential organs are formed during this period.

Similarly, the initial phase of implementing an idea is the most crucial phase, even though it appears nothing is happening. You cannot afford to give up at this stage otherwise you end up losing your reward. However, if you stay the course, you will eventually reap the reward.

E. Ideas can be replaced

The law of cause and effect states that every cause has an effect and every effect has a cause. The results you get in every area of your life are effects whose causes are traceable to the ideas that you have imbibed. Think about it for a minute, the areas of your life where you are achieving success can be directly correlated to the principles you operate in those areas. As a matter of fact, you can reproduce your successes in those areas by applying the same principles again. In the same token, the area of your life where you are getting undesirable results is directly traceable to the ideas that you are applying in that area. To change your results, all you need do is change your ideas. If you change the cause; you will get a different effect. So if for example, you are having relationship problems with your spouse, perhaps what you need to do is to change your idea about how to relate with your spouse. Ideas can be replaced with better ones.

Isn't it amazing to know that you don't have to stick to the same way of doing things because you have always done things in that particular way?

The Process of an Idea

The natural conclusion of an idea is a transformation to its physical form. The transformation however takes a process. In the next couple of pages, I suggest a process through which I believe Ideas can be inspired, developed and implemented. For ease of recall, I have done this using the acronym I.D.E.A.S.

Information

Information births ideas. It is true that the more you know about a particular problem or field of endeavour, the more likely you are to get inspired ideas in that area. I certainly find this to be true for me as a Blogger and Speaker in Leadership and Personal Development. The nature of my work regularly requires that I write new blogs or teach on new subjects. I find that exposing myself to information in my areas of interest regularly gives me new ideas on what next to teach or write about. Take a look at the companies that are thriving today, they are companies that invest heavily into research and development. They constantly seek information on the needs of their clients and devise new ways to meet those needs.

My family and I normally buy most of our groceries from one of the Superstores here in the UK. Some years back, this particular store devised a form of rewards card for their regular customers. Every so often, I received letters in the post from the Superstore with some reward vouchers or discounts for my future shopping with them. At first, I used to receive discounts for random goods that I did not usually require. So I wasn't claiming many of the discounts. Over time, I began to receive discount vouchers for the very goods that I regularly purchased and used. Naturally, I became inclined to using the discount vouchers because it aligned with my needs. I checked with some of my friends whom I knew also use the same Superstore, and they told me they had noticed the same thing.

Clearly this company invested the needed time and effort to research the needs of their individual client. By doing this, they came up with ideas on how to improve their profits by meeting the needs of their clients. That's the power of information in inspiring ideas. Ideas that guarantee success are those that meet needs either by creating something new or improving on what already exists. You need to be aware of events around you to know what needs exist. The awareness of existing needs usually gives birth to ideas.

Shortly after the announcement of the date of the planned wedding between Prince William and the now Duchess of Cambridge, some factories in China started producing and selling wedding souvenirs including a much cheaper plastic version of the engagement ring. The information of the planned event was all that was needed to birth the business idea. So I urge you to open yourself to knowledge in your area of interest. This way, you will always be guaranteed to have ideas that will enable you to make a difference.

Development

Every idea comes at first in a crude form, you need to process and develop it. This stage is about coming up with a clear picture in your mind of your finished product and a strategy for achieving the idea. This stage is the rate limiting process in the transformation of your idea. It requires a lot of time and effort. It is therefore not a surprise that many ideas are abandoned at this stage. This is the stage where you write down your idea, undertake further research and draw a plan to help you achieve your idea. Depending on what you want to achieve, you may need to do a lot more at this stage such as registering a company and obtaining a patent for a product.

At this stage, it is also a good idea to experiment your idea on a small scale. By doing this, you can achieve two things. Firstly, it will provide you information on the viability of your plan and help you identify areas that you need to modify in your plan or if you need to completely re-strategise. Also, it provides the evidence you require for the next stage in the process, which is enlisting.

Enlisting

Now that you are crystal clear in your mind about what you want to do and how you want to do it, it's time to search out for people that can help you bring the idea to fruition. You need to decide the exact roles that the persons you intend to enlist need to play in bringing the idea to fruition. Do you just need investors in your idea? Or do you require their specialised skills? Or are you seeking a partnership? Have you also thought about whether or not your idea would be best served by linking up with an existing service, project or business? It is important to be very clear about what you want.

You also need to get your elevator pitch right, as you don't want to mess up any opportunity that opens up for you. Be prepared to answer the golden question as you will definitely be asked; what's in it for me?

Action

It's now time to go out full steam to implement your idea. Nothing will work unless you do. Work out your idea, advertise your product, and provide the best quality service/product possible. Chances are that you are likely to start small, that's okay. Most things I know start small. If you give every opportunity your best, you are guaranteed to increase.

Stay the course

Whatever happens, don't quit and don't stop believing.

CHAPTER 2

YOUR MOST INVALUABLE ASSET: PEOPLE

Have you ever heard of the appellation 'self-made man or woman'? It is used to describe individuals who despite coming from a disadvantaged background achieve economic success purely from their own hard work and ingenuity rather than from inherited fortunes or family connections. I suspect you may have read a few biographies about such people. I am inspired by the stories of some of these individuals. They provide invaluable lessons in the journey of success. However, I have a fundamental problem with the very word 'self-made' and the definition of the concept. I feel the concept focuses entirely on the individual's role in achieving success. It does not acknowledge the importance of other factors, one of which is people. No doubt, individual factors are very crucial to achieving success. Achieving success however is far from dependent on individual factors only. No one has ever achieved anything significant that did not need the help of people and no one ever will. I challenge you to think of anything significant that has ever been achieved in this world, behind it you will find that people made it happen. People are so crucial to your journey of success. They are your most invaluable asset. John Maxwell sums it up well in this saying:

> "One is too small a number to achieve greatness."

If it is true that you need people to achieve success and significance, the flip side is equally true, people need you to achieve success and significance. Everybody needs somebody. We all need each other. That's the way the world was designed to operate—one big chain of inter-connectivity.

In the film 'Double Platinum' which starred Brandy and Diana Ross, there was a line in the closing song 'Love is all that matters', which reads . . . We all have one heart and one heart needs another. These words are so true. This chapter's focus is about how you can be effective on both sides of your relationship with people. It would address the subject of how you can get the best from people and how you can give you best to people.

Beyond Teamwork—Community

A lot of work has been done by many Leadership and Personal development authorities on the subject of team work and its importance to success. The importance of teamwork to the success of any organisation cannot be understated. However, an individual's biggest influence in life does not come from the team, it comes from the community. A team is often built around a project which has a defined start date and finish date. Team members have clearly defined roles and are mostly paid for fulfilling these roles. In the team, the common goal is over-riding. It's all about achieving the goal. In contrast, a community is often self-organised around a shared value, passion or need. There are no pre-defined roles for people to belong to a community and people are usually not paid to participate in a community. As communities are naturally developed, the ties among the individuals in the community are stronger compared to that of a team. In the community, often motivation is greater as it is derived from a higher social motive such as helping out, having someone else's back and solving a common problem or challenge facing the community. Jim Rohn once said, "You are the average of the five people you spend the most time with."

For many of us, this saying will hold true in our lives. Think about all that you are today and the things that are important to you, most likely you can trace them to the influence of someone who you have or had close ties to. If you grew up in a family where having University education was considered very important, is it any surprise that today as a parent it's important to you that your children get University education? If your closest friends are drug abusers, the chances are that you are already one or you will soon become one.

Time and again, we all encounter individuals who have been able to break the hold of negative influences of their associations on them. We celebrate people who overcome negative backgrounds such as drug habits, gang violence and abuse and grow up to make positive contributions to the world. I guess the reason we celebrate them is because we all know how hard it is to break from the prevailing influence of the community and achieve success. In fact, most of the people who achieve this breakthrough, do so by subscribing to different value systems such as those of a mentor or small group, in order to overcome the prevailing influence of their environment. That's how considerable the community influences every one of us.

The Power of Community

1. **The Community gives you a Value System**

   As already discussed in the preceding paragraphs, an individual derives his/her personal value system from the corporate value system of the community. The family is a child's first community. Every person comes out of a family. The chances are that many of the values that you hold on to today are tied to those you learnt from your family. Basic values that make for successful relationships with others such as courtesy, honesty, integrity are usually developed in childhood in the family. This is the reason the disintegration of the family structure in Britain today is a huge concern. Britain is reputed to have the highest divorce rate in the European Union with a rate of 2.8 per 1,000 people. Similarly, Britain has a rate of 38.8% births outside of marriage. Is it any surprise that about a quarter of Crimes committed in the UK are committed by young people under 18?

2. **The Community helps develop your gifts**

   You are most likely to have first discovered your gift in a community. Somebody somewhere who knew you quite well at some point in time would have first told you that you are quite gifted in a particular area.

Actually you probably only paid attention to the gift after more people from the same community said the same thing about your gift. The chances are that your gifts started finding expression within the same community. You had the benefit of the controlled environment that the community afforded you to perfect your gift and grow it to what it is now. No matter how gifted you are, you need a community to give your gift value.

3. **The Community gives you support**

   In your toughest times, you need all the support and encouragement that you can get. There's no one else who has your back like the community that you belong to. Why? Because your community wants you to succeed as much as you want to, probably even more. Your success is seen as the success of the community, your failure is also seen as the community's failure.

   In the process of chasing your life goals, particularly the challenging ones, you may encounter times where your motivation drops. Facing these kinds of experiences alone can be difficult, and may want to cause you to give up on your goals. However, in a supportive community, you are much more likely to hold on to your goals through the challenging times and ultimately hit them. In the same token, when you feel highly motivated, the entire community can benefit from your positive energy in helping to motivate others.

4. **The Community gives you collective wisdom**

    The Community affords you the opportunity to benefit from the collective wisdom of many people with different skill sets. No matter how smart you are, your wisdom is no match for the collective wisdom of the Community. A Japanese proverb says, "None of us is as smart as all of us."

In a community, new ideas are constantly flowing. This happens because one person's insight and experience inspires the birth of new ideas in others. Also someone is able to build on the work that another person has done in an atmosphere of openness. From my personal experience, I am at my creative best when I am in the company of like-minded people. It's the power of community at work.

5. **The community requires accountability from you**

    So far, I have highlighted several ways in which the community benefits you and a few ways in which you can be of benefit to the community. Perhaps, your greatest responsibility to the Community is accountability. It appears to me that this is one responsibility a lot of people are either not aware of or are unwilling to keep to in today's world. There cannot be a community if the members of the community are not accountable to one another. Each member of the community must be able to give account of their actions and demand accountability from other members of the community. It is a two way thing. Failure to do either leads to a dysfunctional Community.

There is an erroneous concept that I find in today's world that somehow being accountable to others infringes on your individual freedom. This is far from true. True freedom involves being responsible to common laws and values. In fact, the violation of common laws is punishable by the withdrawal of personal rights. If you choose to exercise your personal freedom to decision making by repeatedly violating speed limits, it is only a matter of time before your freedom to drive will be revoked by law. If this holds true in the larger society, why should it not hold true in the Community? Why must the state expect parents to fulfil their responsibility of providing for the needs of their teens and then take the power of decision away from them in certain other areas? This undermines the authority of those who are parents. Why should a young person feel he/she no longer needs to submit to the rules and regulations of his parents but expects them to continue to have parental responsibilities for him/her? It is always a two way thing. When society fails to recognise and enforce either the community's obligations to an individual or an individual's responsibility to the community, then dysfunction is bound to set in. As a nation, we must return to strengthening our families, which are our first communities. Our Nation is only as strong as our family units are.

Principles for successful relationships

1. **Value people**:
   The desire to be valued and treated with dignity is an intrinsic part of being human. Everybody wants to feel worthwhile, everybody wants to be valued. Value is something that you must personally decide to continue to place on people. Everyone deserves to be valued for just being human, regardless of their status or position. If you abide by the golden code of treating

other people as you will prefer to be treated then you are unlikely to go wrong. Be courteous. Always use words like please and thank you in communication. They make a lot of difference to how people respond to you.

One of my teachers in Leadership once urged me to decide that I will never make people feel important, instead to decide that people are important. Yes people are important. Making people feel important is like play acting, but deciding that people are important will make you always treat people with importance.

This is one major lesson I believe that Leaders in the Developing World need to learn. I once gave a hard thought to the question of the major difference between the Developed World and the Developing World. I did this as someone who has experienced living in both Worlds and I came to one conclusion. The conclusion is that both the Leadership and the Systems in the Developing World unlike in the Developed World do not value people.

I could give you several examples to illustrate this. Do I discuss the 500,000 women that die as a result of pregnancy related causes every year in Sub-Saharan Africa and have been doing so for at least 10 years? What possible excuse could the Governments and Leadership in these Nations have for not checking this disastrous trend for so long? Do I discuss the several thousands of lives that are lost in Road Traffic Accidents every year in the Developing World and not much has been done to reduce this trend for so long?

It is about time we realised that the human life is the most precious commodity on this planet, once lost, it cannot be regained. People who are remembered many years after their death are not remembered for what they had, but for what they did with what they had. Gain some wisdom from one of the richest men of our time, Bill Gates. In his recent speech to graduates of Harvard University, he had this to say, "Humanity's greatest advances are not in its discoveries, but in how those discoveries are applied to reduce inequities".

It's high time all who occupy leadership positions in the Developing World and all who aspire to these positions in the near future started to re-consider their priorities. We must start valuing people.

2. Have integrity with people

Integrity is the quality of being true to yourself and the principles that you adhere to at all times. It should be your guiding principle for relating with everyone. People must be able to trust that every word that comes out of your mouth is the truth. You must not leave anyone in doubt as to the quality of your character.

Unfortunately, integrity is no longer common place today, even amongst our leaders. The recent event of the Members of Parliament's expenses scandal in the UK is still fresh in our minds. There are times that I feel that it must be quite confusing for young people growing in today's society to decide on what's the right way to live, seeing there is a lot of mismatch of speech and character. Even some of the regular TV shows don't help in this regard. However, relating with other people with integrity is the right way to live. You owe it to yourself to live right. Imagine how much effort a person needs to put into remembering all they say at all times because they know they are telling a lie. That's just too much stress to put up with. Living a life of integrity saves you all that stress because you know that you always say the truth, so don't have to put an extra effort into remembering all that you say.

3. Pay it forward

I borrowed this header from one of my favourite Hollywood movies of all time by the same title, which starred Kevin Spacey, Helen Hunt and Haley Joel Osment. In the movie, a social studies teacher gives his seventh grade class an assignment to come up with a plan to change the world for better. In response, an eleven year old boy named Trevor devises a brilliant plan which he called 'Pay it forward'. According to his plan, he starts a chain of doing favours for 3 persons, and the recipients of the favour in turn are expected to do favours for 3 other people rather than return the favour. By doing this, he hoped to set up a branching chain of favours which will eventually change the world. Eventually despite some challenges, his plan worked. He changed the world in his own little way.

Why do you want to be successful? You probably have a thousand and one reasons for wanting to succeed. Do your reasons include making a difference in the lives of other people and making the world a better place? If not, think again. Success that does not influence others positively is not true success. Influencing others for good is something you need to deliberately get involved in. It does not matter whether you are rich or poor, highly or lowly placed, regardless of your current situation, you can make somebody's life better. Your life is the answer to somebody's question. Right now, somebody somewhere is waiting for your help to survive, will you deny them?

Start paying it forward today. Lend a helping hand to that neighbour who desperately needs your help. Register with a charity and continue to give to worthwhile causes. Did you know that with as little as £2 a month (less than the price of one meal) you can change another person's life in another part of the world for good? You don't need to have enough or a lot to be able to give. Giving is the way to receive.

A person who attends to the needs of others will always find help in his/her own time of need. No man is an island; you will always need others to do one thing or another for you; however little. As you pay it forward to others, it is only a matter of time before someone pays it forward to you.

It is my firm belief that as you apply these principles to tap into the power of the Community, you will significantly increase your odds of succeeding in life. People are indeed your most invaluable asset, value people and your life will appreciate in value.

CHAPTER 3

YOUR MOST DEPLOYABLE ASSET: MONEY

King Solomon, the wisest man who ever lived once said that, "Money solves a lot of problems." Zig Ziglar also says, "Money is not everything, but it ranks right up there with oxygen." By implication, money is the one resource that you can deploy to address many problems in life. No other resource in life addresses as many problems as money does. It is an essential resource for success.

By strict definition, no one is born with money, however, everyone is born with a capacity to earn and create money. This capacity to create money is one of the best things in life, and it is free. How much money a person ends up having, is a factor of how well that person has developed his/her capacity to create, multiply and manage wealth. Orison Swett Marden puts it succinctly, "The greatest thing a man can do in this world is to make the most possible out of the stuff that has been given him. This is success, and there is no other."

Fundamentally, there are 3 ways in which success is measured in today's world:

1. Where you occupy (Position)

The first way success is measured is by what position a person holds or has held in the past. For many people who seek success through a career path, this is often the way in which they would define success. As an example, a person in the academia may define success as attaining to the level of becoming a professor in a field of interest. A politician may define success as becoming a Governor, Senator or President. A medical doctor will be regarded as successful after becoming a consultant. At this level, success is all about the position attained.

2. What you have done (Impact)

A second way in which success can be measured is by what a person has done. This is usually a measure of a person's impact in a particular field. Awards like the Nobel Prize are intended to celebrate success in this area. Whilst a person's position may determine the extent of their impact, a person does not have to hold a high position to make an impact. People like the late Mother Teresa and Tawakel Karman are examples of individuals who have made considerable impact without holding a high position.

3. What you have (Assets)

Another way in which Success is measured is by how much assets a person possesses. This is usually done through converting all the material possessions of an individual into the cash equivalent. The resultant value is then used as a measure of that person's wealth. This conversion allows a comparison of wealthy individuals across the world. This is how a list of the top richest individuals in the world is produced on an annual basis.

Whilst it is impossible to say that any of these three categories of success is better than the other, it could be argued that individuals in the third category can achieve success in the other two categories if they want to. However, the converse is not always the case. To illustrate this point, many of the foundations making a difference in the world today are visions of wealthy entrepreneurs of their time. In fact, the funds and grants given out by these organisations are direct products of the investment of the monetary assets of these visionaries. As a result, many of these lives such as John D. Rockefeller, Henry Ford and Andrew Carnegie continue to influence several millions of people even today, many years after their death. By the same token, wealthy individuals are very often desired by many organisations for leadership positions in their organisations, because of what they bring to the table.

The message here is simple, if you must become successful in life, you must understand the nature and purpose of money, and how to multiply it. This ability lies innate in you; however, you must activate it through the right type of financial education.

Understanding the nature of Money

Money is a neutral entity that has the ability to take on the nature of the person possessing it. It is neither good nor bad intrinsically, however it has the capacity to become either, depending on whose hands it's in. A lot of good has been done in the world with money. By the same token, a lot of evil has been perpetrated using money as a resource. It all depends on whose hands the money is in.

Similarly, money has the capacity to take the position of a master or servant depending on which position is adopted by its possessor. It can either work for a person or a person can work for it. It's all a factor of understanding and choice. Every day, I see many people serving money rather than have money serve them. Money dictates when they wake up, when they eat, when they go to bed and when they take a holiday. Money dictates that they need to do two jobs. It dictates how much time they get to spend with their family. Please do not confuse being an employee with serving money. It is not always the case. A person can remain employed at a job out of the satisfaction of doing that job, whilst still having money work for her or him through investments. The fundamental difference is whether a person works primarily to pay the bills or whether this is a secondary interest.

Robert Kiyosaki in his book Rich Dad, Poor Dad, argues that one of the fundamental differences between the Rich and the Poor is that rich people have money work for them, while poor people work for money. However, it takes understanding money in a different light to what is conventionally taught in formal educational institutions to achieve this.

Money is a type of currency, which in its most basic form implies a means of exchange. The word currency is derived from the word 'Current'. A current is characterised by a flow, examples include electrical currents and ocean currents. Similarly, money flows, it's never static. It flows from you to others and from others to you. What determines your net-worth is which direction the flow is highest. If more money flows from you than does to you, then you will be poor. However, if more money flows to you than does from you, you will be rich.

To keep the flow of money to you higher than the flow of money from you, requires financial literacy. Many of the principles that keep the flow of money to you higher than the flow away from you are not rocket science. They are actually basic things. I will be discussing some of them over the next few pages.

How to manage and increase your cash flow

1. Control your appetite

Cyril Northcote Parkinson in 1955 articulated a law which has famously become known as Parkinson's Law. It states that 'work expands so as to fill the time available for its completion.' Over the years an aphorism of that law has evolved which is equally true. It states that 'expenses always rise to meet up with income.' Think for a minute; is this law at work in you? What happened to your last pay rise? Did it translate to savings and investment, or did it translate to luxury? Why is it that despite several pay rises, you still get to spend every penny earned and still require more? This is Parkinson's Law at work. Naturally, the human appetite is insatiable. It has to be controlled if you must have any chance of becoming wealthy. For example, you don't have to buy a bigger house because you can now afford it, if your current house is serving you well. The extra income should rather go into the service of working for you by earning more. This is the first and probably most important secret to wealth. Learn to live below your means.

2. Sow seeds into the future

Farmers follow the principles of seed time and harvest to be able to guarantee provisions for themselves and their families in the future. From every harvest, they take out the seeds to be sown now, in order to guarantee another harvest in the future. It would be unwise for a farmer to eat up all of his harvest. The only predictable result of this action is that he/she will be out of business in the near future.

If this illustration looks reasonable to you, is it not also reasonable that a certain fraction of your income goes into the future as seeds in order to guarantee you a harvest? You may say I already do that, I contribute into a pension fund. To that I'll respond well done . . . , but that's not enough.

If you have been following events around the globe lately, you will understand that major reforms of the pension scheme are taking place in some of the advanced countries of the world. Here in the UK, changes have been proposed and in some cases, are already being implemented to the pension scheme. By the proposed plan, in the future, people will be working longer, contributing more to pensions and earning less eventually when they retire. This proposal has met with several protests by trade unions and more recently, a strike action by doctors (first of its kind in about 40 years). It is my considered opinion that no amount of strike will stop the implementation of similar plans, not only in the UK but across the world. It is an inevitable event as most Governments are cracking under the weight of pensions, as life expectancy increases across the globe.

To put this into perspective; in 1990 in the UK, a man who reached the pensionable age of 65 years was expected to spend 15.9 years in retirement. A woman, who also reached the age of 65 years in 1990, was expected to spend about

19.4 years in retirement. Based on estimates from 2010, men and women reaching the pensionable age of 65 years in 2011 are expected to spend 21.1 and 23.8 years in retirement respectively. That's a difference of 5.2 years and 5.4 years for men and women respectively in about 20 years.

Now imagine the state bearing the responsibility of paying pension to hundreds of thousands to millions of individuals for that time period. Clearly, reforms are needed to the current pension scheme if it must remain sustainable. It's therefore not a surprise that individuals are required to work longer and contribute more to earn lesser in the future. You need a plan that puts your future directly under your control and not any Government or Institution. This is the only way to guarantee success both in the now and in the times to come.

Here is my suggestion of an investment plan into the future. It's called the 20% investment rule, based on the principle enunciated by the biblical Joseph in the ancient civilisation of Egypt. ". . . take a fifth of the harvest of Egypt during the seven years of abundance . . . This food should be held in reserve for the country, to be used during the seven years of famine . . ." The principle is; 20% of today's earning should be invested into the future. I love this principle because it is not about an amount but about a proportion. Here are some other reasons why I think this is a good plan:

   a. **It was a world changing plan**: "And all the countries came to Egypt to buy grain from Joseph, because the famine was severe in the entire world."

   Although Joseph's plan was instituted in Egypt, it ended up saving the whole world, as the famine cut across all the nations. Very few people in their life time get to impact a nation talk more of the entire world. It doesn't get any better than this.

   b. **Times change but principles don't**: although Joseph's plan was instituted thousands of years ago, the same principles if applied properly will guarantee success today. Men are time bound, but principles are timeless.

Your instinct will be to argue that you can't afford it. My response will be for you to ask yourself whether or not you are a victim of the Parkinson's Law? If you are, I will put it simply again, cut off whatever is unnecessary until that proportion is available for your future. If you have to change your car, do it. If you have to downgrade your house to cut expenses, do it. No present convenience is worth the price of your future. If however, you genuinely find it difficult to achieve this proportion, then start where you are and plan to increase the proportion regularly until you can meet this target or exceed it. Whatever you do, make sure something is being invested into your future. There are several types of investments, stocks, bonds, real estate, green investments, the list goes on. You may want to take the advice of a financial adviser in this regard.

3. Sensible borrowing

I think it is a wonderful thing that in today's world, there is a banking system in place to help people get loans to enable them to meet some of their needs. The down side to this however, is that many individuals get loans for many of their wants and not necessarily needs. The consequence of this is that a lot of people perpetually live in debt, which significantly compromises how much money they have available to invest into their future. The solution therefore to preventing a life of debt is the concept of sensible borrowing.

Sensible borrowing implies that you only borrow when the purpose for the borrowed sum is to multiply the amount borrowed in order to make a profit. This would include borrowing to start a business, borrowing to make an investment, in which the projected profit is higher than the interest to be paid to the lender. Sensible borrowing is not borrowing to meet your immediate or personal needs. It certainly is not borrowing for pleasure.

If you give a thought to this definition, you will find that the most common reasons for which people borrow money does not fit within the context of sensible borrowing. Borrowing today is driven by culture rather than logic. Why get a loan to drive a car that you cannot afford? By the time, you are done repaying the loan, guess what? It's time to change the car, and the culture of indebtedness continues. Just in case you were wondering, the use of credit cards is also a form of loan. So the principle of sensible borrowing needs to apply to what you use your credit cards to pay for.

Sensible borrowing is what a significant number of rich individuals and corporations including banks tap into, to multiply their assets. Sensible borrowing includes loans, equities, franchises and partnerships. With the exception of loans, these other forms of financing enable other people to buy into not only your business, but to also take on part of the risk. They are still very viable options for starting businesses even in these times.

4. Understand the financial system

Financial systems differ from country to country. In order to take the best advantage of the system in which you live, it's imperative that you understand the operating financial system. In developed countries of the world, one of the first things you need to understand is the credit scoring system and how it is derived. In my experience, this is not usually a problem for long term residents of these countries. However, it can be a huge problem for those who immigrate especially from developing countries of the world.

The credit scoring system is a system used to rate credit applicants on the basis of several characteristics, in order to determine their credit worthiness. The higher you score, the more credit worthy you are considered to be. The lower you score, the less credit worthy you are considered to be. Note that a credit scoring system does not judge your credit worthiness on the basis of how much you have avoided getting in debt. On the contrary, it judges your ability to pay back what you borrow on the basis of how you have paid back borrowed money in the past.

Things that will aid you in getting a good credit score include getting on the electoral roll at your address, timely payment of bills, timely payment of direct debits and credit card repayments. For those who may have only recently migrated to a developed country, the credit card is a very useful instrument to building your credit history. A word of caution however, is to use the card without getting into debt. The principle I applied when I first arrived the UK, was to do all of my normal monthly spending on my credit card, and make my repayments in full. This afforded me the chance to build my credit history rather quickly without incurring any debt in the process.

Another aspect of the financial system you need to understand is the importance of making above minimum payments. For the purpose of illustration, if we assume that a person takes out a mortgage of £199, 500 to purchase a house at an annual percentage rate of 4.5%, over a term of 25 years. If that person commits to making an extra payment of £100 per month from the start of the mortgage, (s)he would end up paying off the mortgage 3 and ½ years earlier and saving about £21, 134 in interest. It gets better, if that person decides to increase the overpayment to £200 per month from the start of the same mortgage, (s)he would end up repaying the mortgage 6 years earlier and save £36, 256 in interest. This is the beauty of understanding the financial system in which you live. I know that the reality is that many people re-mortgage after fixed periods depending on the prevailing interest rates. That regardless, the practice of over-payment substantially reduces how much you pay back.

S.M.A.R.T TIPS FOR SUCCESS

5. Put your greatest gift to use

All other factors being constant, your greatest income earner is putting your greatest gift to use. The world is full of stories of people who stood out in different fields of human endeavours through recognising and deploying their gifts. From the world of entertainment, to the world of sports all the way through to politics, history is replete with story after story of people who became outstanding by putting their greatest gift to use.

In the book 'Gifted Hands', the autobiography of Dr Benjamin Carson, Dr Carson himself outlines how his greatest gifts, which are a good eye-hand coordination and the ability to reason in three dimensions have made him an outstanding Neuro-surgeon. To date, he has recorded significant successes in the field of paediatric neurosurgery. Notable among his achievements are the first successful separation of Siamese twins conjoined at the back of the head and the first successful placement of an intra-uterine shunt for a hydrocephalic twin. These achievements have not only brought him success and influence within the medical community, but beyond. As of today, he has received numerous awards including the Presidential Medal of Freedom in 2008 (highest civilian award in the United States) and has four bestselling books to his credit. Dr Carson is a true example of how using your greatest gifts can be a true source of wealth and influence.

Here are a few reasons why I believe that a man's greatest gift when deployed is his greatest income earner.

1. **Your proficiency in your greatest gift is above average**: naturally, in the area of your natural gifting, you already stand out of the pack. You'll know this because other people tell you. I first knew I was gifted in speaking when every time I gave a public talk, people always gave me a feedback of how good they felt my speaking ability was. In order to become outstanding in the area of your greatest gifting, further training and practice is usually required. However, because it is an area of natural gifting to you, improvements come rather quickly and with less effort. So in terms of time and cost, the investment needed to develop the gift to an outstanding level is much lower, compared to someone else whose gifting in the same area is average. The returns on the other hand are huge.

2. **The more outstanding, the more the attraction**: the more outstanding a person's gift is, the more people are willing to pay to access that person's gift. Take the soccer world for example, within the same club, some

players earn up to 10 times what other players earn. The more gifted players attract higher incomes while their less gifted colleagues, attract lesser income. It is simply the way the world operates.

3. **Great gifts attract multiple incomes**: highly talented people are often sought after beyond their field of interest. A lot of the times, companies and corporations count on their influence in other areas to help the particular company's sales. This is the reason, companies use highly talented individuals in the field of entertainment and sports for TV and internet adverts for their products.

In the build up to the men's Wimbledon 2012 final, some journalists estimated that Andy Murray's asset could easily soar from about £24 million to £100 million by winning the men's final. By being the first British man to win a Wimbledon championship in 76 years, the expectation was that in addition to playing tennis, he could easily make more money by branching in to cloth lines, tennis or health clubs. Unfortunately, this was not to be the case as Andy Murray lost the final match to Roger Federer. Andy would eventually go on to win the Gold medal in Tennis at the Olympics and the US Tennis Open championship later that year.

The tragedy of our time is that a lot of people are not deploying their greatest gift, or may be at best are deploying it as a hobby. Most people spend their time doing something else to make a living. How many writers in our world today are busy doing something completely irrelevant to writing? How many gifted people in painting are today working in the science laboratory? No one has ever been known to excel from a position of weakness. Build your career around your strength and not your weakness. It sounds so simple, however you will be amazed at how many people do the opposite i.e. try to tailor their strengths to their careers. Many times the driving force behind this is survival.

You can only be exceptional if you continue to do things that you are uniquely wired for. Yes it's true that you may need a job to survive and sometimes you may not have much control over which kind of jobs you get initially. What becomes a tragedy is if you choose to stay in the same situation all your life and not use your present situation as a platform to get what you truly want. To reverse the situation may require you to change jobs or start something entirely new. It may also require you to go for different roles within the same institution. For example, you may not like your current role in a bank; however you are passionate about investment banking. Have you thought of undertaking a course in investment banking and applying for a change of unit? Dare to be different.

A word on Student Loans

The principle of making investments into the future should not just be for yourself alone, you must seriously consider including your children in that plan. In the UK, as with other developed countries, student loans have been a source of financing for the education of many who would otherwise not have been able to do so. I think the student loan system is wonderful. Thanks to the scheme, today, hundreds of thousands of people have a University Qualification and an appropriately matched job.

Recently, the UK Government raised the upper limit of university tuition fees to a maximum of £9, 000 per annum, nearly 300% of the previous upper limit. It is envisaged that many Universities will raise their tuition fees to the maximum. All parents who plan for their children to access these student loans in the future need to consider the following:

a. It is likely that the benchmark for student loans will still be raised in the future.

b. As the benchmarks for student loan increase, so will the debt deepen for as many as access it.

Using the current benchmark as an illustration, a student who obtains a loan of £9,000 per annum for tuition fee and £3,575 as annual maintenance fee, for a 3 year undergraduate course will repay just over £56,000 over a period of 24 and ½ years, assuming a starting salary of £25,000. Now imagine that person getting married to another graduate, who also accessed the student loan. That's a combined debt of over £100,000 from the very start of the marriage. Clearly, that's a recipe for a challenging life together.

As a parent however, you can start early by making long term savings and investments for your children towards their university education. For example, if you have a child who is under 5 years of age now, you have the opportunity of at least 13 years to make investments towards the university education of that child. You will be amazed at how little investments made regularly over a long period of time compounds. You may want to discuss with your financial adviser about the various options available to allow you do this.

A guide on how to become debt free

As I previously highlighted in the preceding chapter, debt is a major hindrance to many people investing into their future. The culture of living in debt has become accepted as inevitable by many. However, there is nothing inevitable about living in debt. With a little bit of discipline and planning, anyone with a regular means of income can become debt free. Here I discuss a simple guide to becoming debt free. Please note that I have not taken a mortgage into account for this illustration, as generally mortgages are significantly larger than other forms of debts and take longer to settle. However, many of the principles illustrated here will also apply to settling your mortgage.

a. Take an account of all the debt you owe. This will include loans from banks, borrowings you made from friends and family and outstanding credit card payments.

b. Determine how much you need to pay back on a regular basis (most likely monthly or weekly basis). On the basis of this, set an objective for when you want to become debt free based on your affordability.

c. Decide that you will make no further borrowings. This is just common sense. You don't want to keep increasing debt whilst at the same time planning to become debt free.

d. Shop the market for loans with low interest. Today's market is full of deals. It is as if banks are out-competing themselves for who can give the best deal. A word of caution; when going for deals with interest rates lower than your current loan, make your decision on the basis of overall outstanding repayment and not just monthly repayment. In some cases, monthly repayments are lesser, however, depending on the term of the loan; you may end up paying more back than if you had stayed with your current arrangements.

e. Shop the market for zero percent balance transfers on credit cards. These deals are only good deals if you continue to make some repayments during the period that the zero percent interest applies. Otherwise, you will find that you may need to make more repayments than you had envisaged at the end of the deal period.

f. Follow a strict budget and determine that you will cut down your monthly expenses by 5-10%. This extra should go into savings and investments. The reason many people fall into debt is the lack of a back-up plan for the rainy day. So, when financial emergencies arise, the only thing to fall back on is getting a loan. You can however avoid that by regularly setting aside a percentage of your income for savings and investment.

g. Split any unexpected income into two—one half for savings, the other to be committed to paying off your debts. Every once a while, you will get some additional income that you did not expect, such as a cheque from the tax office or income that is outside your normal income such as working extra hours. Whilst in indebtedness, this money is not to be spent for pleasure. It should be committed to the process of becoming debt free.

h. Explore other means of generating income by applying all the principles discussed so far.

CHAPTER 4

YOUR MOST INFLEXIBLE ASSET: TIME

Time is truly one of the most important assets that anyone can possess. The best thing about time is that it is free. Not only is time a free resource, it is given to every person in equal measure per day. It is the only resource that you can truly say that everyone has got in equal measure. I know that a lot of people are familiar with the last statement, but I don't feel that as many people think about what the sentence truly means. For a minute, I want you to pause and think about the statement—everyone has got time in equal measure. Successful and unsuccessful people, rich and poor, young and old, male and female, single or married, everyone has got time in equal measure. However the outcomes that people get in life are in no way equal. Amongst many other differences, one of the major differences between successful and unsuccessful people is how much value they attach to time and how they use their time. I will elaborate further on this in the succeeding pages of this chapter.

Understanding the Concept of Time

The concept of time can be viewed from two broad perspectives. The first is the concept of time as a continuum extending from the past to the present through to the future in which events happen in an irreversible progression. Using this understanding, time can be quantified using numbers in various units ranging from seconds to years. This is the commonest way in which we often refer to the concept of time.

The second concept groups time into an interval period for the purpose of describing a specific purpose or event. This concept is what we generally refer to when we talk about seasons, an era, or an age of human existence such as the industrial age. This concept is also what is used to describe various stages of human existence such as childhood, adolescence, adulthood and old age. Interpreting time in this way helps us make more sense of life in a different way to how we can using the numeric concept of time. For an individual to make the most effective use of time, it is important to understand and apply time in these two different ways.

The Importance of Time

Why is time so important? It is important for the following reasons.

a. **Time is Life**

    Time is the unit in which life is measured. Every single thing that a person does, achieves or becomes in life is done in time. Think about this, when a person is born, they are born with only two resources; time and an undeveloped mind. In the process of time, that person exchanges the resource of time for the development of the mind, through the help of people. Eventually, the developed mind is partly exchanged for money, in the form of a job, a service or a product to sell. That money is what is used in turn to acquire whatever that person eventually possesses. In essence, what the person has done is exchange part of his life (his time) for whatever he may now have become or acquired. This is the reason some people say that time is money. This is partly true, the bigger picture actually is that time is life.

b. **Time is Limited**

    Time unlike all the other assets that a person freely possesses is truly a limited resource. There is nothing that anyone can do to increase or reduce time. It is a person's most inflexible asset. Unlike the Economic definition of a fixed asset, which is an asset that is not consumed during the normal course of business (for example land, equipments, building), time is an asset that is automatically consumed. It is that inflexible. This quality of time is what underscores the importance of deliberately making the most effective use of your time. Either you use time wisely or not, it continues to count. Right now as you read this book, time is counting. There is nothing you can do to ever regain the last second. Either you utilised it or not, it's gone forever.

c. **Time is the medium for growth**
Most things in life, animate and inanimate grow with time, humans inclusive. For as long as life persists, growth continues. In the process of time, virtually any skill can be learnt and perfected. In time, novices become experts, a child becomes an adult and small businesses become mega industries; everything happens in time. This understanding of time should reassure you that it is never too late to start a venture as long as you have got time. Stop complaining of how your life would have been so much better, if only

you had more formal education. All you need is time and that you have got, because you are still alive.

d. Time is not forever

You need to understand that for you, time is not forever. A time will come when either by reason of frailty or death, you will not be able to do the things that you can now do. This is why it's important to apply yourself as much as you can to maximising each day now that you can. Stop always thinking that you have got another day to do what you should do today, because you may not. This is the evil of procrastination.

Conventionally, procrastination is described as putting off an action to a later time when you could equally have done it at that particular time. However, if you think of procrastination in the context of effective use of time, it is more than just putting off an action. It is the term you use to describe an action or event that has missed its time. In other words, you have wasted the original time that was allotted to doing that action or event. Time works with your decisions. It is not enough to desire or wish that you do something. What gives meaning to time is what you decide to do per time and acting on it.

Principles for Managing Time

World's famous leadership guru John Maxwell believes that there is no such thing as time management. He argues that there is nothing you can do in any way to change time, it keeps counting. What you can manage however is your life. I totally agree with John. How you use your time is a measure of how you use your life. This is consistent with the earlier assertion that your time is your life. That stated, how can you manage your life to give the best value to time?

   a. **Have a Purpose for Time**
      The importance of time is in the purpose attached to it. So in order to manage time, you need to assign a purpose to it. Purpose in this respect can be viewed from two perspectives. First perspective is to see purpose from the point of view of your life mission. What is it you were born to do and what can you do now to achieve that? When you know the answer to this question, your overall time can be spent within the context of what is important for the achievement of your purpose. Lee Iacocca says, "If you want to make good use of your time, you've got to know what's most important and then give it all you've got."

Time spent on achieving your life purpose is time well spent. For example, I love speaking and writing. I believe they are part of the things I was born to do. As a result, I invest a good part of my time in both speaking and writing, and in activities that enhance my skills in these areas. This is time well spent because it is time spent on my life purpose.

The second context in which purpose can be seen is the context of what specific purpose you have assigned to a particular time. Ideally this should be in the light of your larger life purpose. The reason this point is important however is that there are several things you could do per time, all of which could enhance your overall purpose. However, you could not possibly do all of these things at the same time. This is the reason you need to attach a specific purpose to your time. The activity which you assign to a specific time period is the most important thing to do to maximise that time. At any other time, the particular activity may not be important. For example, if you have allotted a specific time as family time, the most important thing you could do at that time is spend that time with family. Any other time, reading a book may be more important, but not at the time you have allotted to spend with family.

b. **Be organised**

    Believe it or not, one of the biggest wasters of time is looking for missing items. From my personal experience, in some instances, it can take up to several hours over several days to find something that I have misplaced. After some years, I have finally come to realise that I could do a lot more things with the time I waste looking for missing items. And the key for me was to become more organised in how I arrange my stuffs. Now, I personally use designated and well labelled storage areas. So if I need a document or item, straight away, I know where it's likely to be. This is just an example of how being organised can help you manage your life better.

    You can also be better organised in the planning of your activities. It could be a good idea to plan your entire week ahead, obviously allowing some free time for unexpected developments. What you do not want to certainly do is waking up and taking each day as it comes. If you do that, the chances are you will end up spending a lot of time doing other people's agenda. If however you have planned your entire day or week ahead, you know exactly how much time you have to spare to help others achieve their own agenda.

c.   **Be Proactive**

As I previously stated, time already spent can never be regained. However, you can decide ahead what you want to do per time. To do this requires being proactive. To put it simply, there are things that you will always need to do. Being proactive is thinking ahead about those things that you need to do and working out the best way to do them, that saves you the most time. As an example, you know that you will need to pay your utility bills every month, why do you have to go to a street store every month to pay your bills when you can simply set up a direct debit? It does not cost any more or less to pay by direct debit; however think of how much time you could save over a year by using the direct debit method. This same principle can be extended to many other aspects of your life—servicing your car regularly to prevent an unwanted breakdown, regular exercise to prevent a health breakdown that could cost you some time off work and spending time with your children to prevent attending to behavioural crisis in the future.

d.   **Understand the Seasons of Life**

You would recall that I stated earlier that time can also be described in terms of the seasons of life. Life seasons come with responsibilities and opportunities. There are some things best done in their season, simply because it can be difficult to do them at other times. As a matter of fact, doing some things outside of their season may not bring about the same result as when they are done in their season. For example, a farmer who misses the season of sowing can sow his seeds at any other time. The only problem is that he is unlikely to reap the same magnitude of harvest. Essentially, seasons dictate what activities need doing. If you are a parent with young children as an example, this is the season to bond and form a relationship with them, whilst they live with you and still very inclined to spending time with you. A time will come when they would no longer live in the same house as you. Even if they still live in the same house with you, they may not just be inclined to wanting to spend as much time with you. At that point, you may have just missed the season.

As another example, there is a season to work; it's called the years of productivity. A season of life comes when you cannot be gainfully employed even if you want to. It's all about the season dictating what the priority for that time is.

There are other seasons that are not strictly speaking natural seasons. They are seasons that we create for ourselves, but are none the less equally important as the natural seasons. It may be a season to do a particular project or attend to a particular problem. The most likely thing is that most of your effort and time is directed towards the project at the time. As an illustration, I had to spend a lot of time to write this book. At the time, I had to forego quite a number of things to finish this project within the stipulated time. In my opinion, it's a good use of time and life. On the flip side, seasons don't last forever, so you are not stuck in doing the same thing over and over again. My point essentially is that a good use of time is doing the required actions that come with every season in life.

e. Delegate responsibilities

You give value to time when you delegate appropriately. Appropriate delegation is allowing the person with the best skillset for a particular task to do that task. That person will not only do it better but faster. More importantly, the need to re-visit the same action is nullified because you have let the best person for the job do it.

Like most people living in the developed world, I had always believed that it's cheaper to do my house repairs myself than contract out the job to a Handyman. I preferred to take out some time as leave from work to do the job if necessary. Whilst speaking with one of my friends and colleague recently on this subject, he shared some insights with me in this regard which has altered my whole perspective on the subject of D.I.Y. He said to me, "do you know as a professional you earn more money per hour doing what you do best, than using the same hour doing house repairs, which you are not very good at. On the other hand, the Handyman is better trained for the job of house repairs. He would do it faster and better than you would do it yourself. The best part is that you will pay the handyman less an hour than you will make if you were at work at that time". That's the power of delegation.

Time and Opportunity

Perhaps the best thing about time is the opportunities it brings along. Every season in life has its own opportunities. There is no season in life; either good or bad, that is devoid of opportunities. The challenge often is that we don't see the opportunities inherent in the seasons. The wisest man who ever lived had this to say about time and opportunity:

> "Yet another thing I observed under the sun is that races aren't won by the swift or battles by the strong and that food doesn't go to the wise or wealth to the intelligent or favour to the experts; rather, time and chance rule them all."

King Solomon raises an important subject in this text. He rightly observed that success in any area of human endeavour is not always predictable by the natural skill or endowment of the person or group of persons involved. Ordinarily, you will expect the fastest man to win the race; you will expect the more intelligent people to be the ones to attract the greatest riches and a man of wisdom to be able to meet his own needs. However, he submits that the common denominators that determine whether or not people of natural endowment meet with success are the factors of time and opportunity (otherwise called chance). In fact, he says these factors rule over all the others. It is therefore important to understand how these concepts play a role in achieving success and how to take advantage of them where possible.

Time in this context relates to a season or a set time or an allotted time for a specific purpose. Every season is set for a purpose and every purpose has a set time. Chance in this context is an opportunity to do something in time or a season. Just as in nature, different seasons have different purposes and therefore different opportunities. For example, every crop has an ideal season in which it needs to be planted. Planting outside of this season does not yield the same result. Similarly, life seasons come with different opportunities. To be successful, you must learn to decipher which opportunities are right for the season in which you are and seize them.

From my personal study and experience, I have come to understand that it always takes the combination of time and chance to get the intended result (all other factors being constant). To expand on this line of thought, think about a successful person, group or organisation that you know, they became successful by seizing an opportunity to do something that the time was right for. The rightness of time often manifests in the readiness of the people targeted to accept the product, service or idea in question. If any of these two factors is not in place, then success cannot be achieved.

History is replete with stories of people who attempted to seize opportunities when the time was not right. It is also replete with stories of people who did not seize opportunities even though the time was right. The outcome of both situations is that success is not achieved or delayed until such a time as both factors align. You may have heard of some ideas that were described as 'ideas ahead of time'. In my considered opinion, this is a descriptive term for ideas that their proponents saw an opportunity to do something; however the timing was not right, because the people were not ready to receive their ideas. On the flip side, the term 'missed opportunities' is used to describe opportunities that were not taken even though the timing was right. Let's consider an example of each of these scenarios from the archives of history, first an example of an idea ahead of its time.

A code not de-coded on time

The Universal Product Code (UPC), a form of bar codes is today being used by millions of companies across the World to identify consumer products. The Uniform Code Council, which is the body responsible for issuing the codes estimates that UPC symbols are scanned about 5 billion times a day. Such is the magnitude of use of the UPC today that it is difficult to imagine how businesses would thrive without it. As a matter of fact, in the days before the UPC was introduced, large stores and supermarkets had to shut down their businesses mostly once a month to count all their stocks manually. With this background, it is difficult to see how the idea of the UPC would not have been jumped at by anyone at that time. Surprisingly, this was exactly what happened. It took about 22 years from the time the bar code was patented to its first commercial use.

The idea for today's bar code was first inspired by an event in 1948 in which Bernard Silver, a graduate student of Philadelphia's Drexel Institute of Technology overheard a conversation in the halls of the Institution. In the conversation, the president of a food chain was pleading with one of the deans to undertake research on automating supermarkets' grocery checkout process. The dean turned down the request, but Silver mentioned the conversation to his friend Norman Joseph Woodland. Woodland was at that time a twenty-seven-year-old graduate student and teacher at Drexel. This idea fascinated Woodland and both himself and Silver decided to undertake research into this problem.

Several months later after a lot of work, Woodland came up with the linear bar code using elements from the Morse code and Movie Soundtracks. The inspiration for the bar code design came to Woodland whilst relaxing by the beach considering how to solve the problem. He unconsciously stuck his fingers in the sand and raked a set of parallel lines that looked like a kind of "long form" of dots and dashes.

Those lines birth the idea of the bar-code design that he and Silver ultimately patented in 1952. By this time Woodland was already an employee of IBM. In the late 50s, Woodland pushed for IBM to consider hiring a Consultant to evaluate the potential of bar code. The Consultant surmised that although bar codes had great possibilities, the technology required to commercialize the concept was at least 5 years away.

In the years that followed, IBM offered a couple of times to buy the patent from Woodland and Silver. However, both Woodland and Silver would not sell to IBM because they thought the price offered was less than the patent was worth. Eventually, a company called Philco met their price and bought the patent off Woodland and Silver in 1962. Silver died a year later. Philco later sold the patent to the Radio Corporation of America (RCA).

RCA commissioned a special group to continue to research into bar code technology. Eventually RCA developed a bulls-eye bar code system which it demonstrated at a grocery industry meeting in 1971. The meeting attracted quite a large turn-out. IBM executives at that meeting noticed the crowds RCA had attracted and became worried that they were losing out on a potentially huge market. One of IBM's marketing specialist recalled that Woodland—whose patent had expired in 1969 was still a staff at IBM. Woodland was soon relocated to IBM's facilities in North Carolina, where he played a key role in developing the UPC version of the bar code. IBM's UPC version of the bar code was eventually adopted by the Grocery Industry in April, 1973.

On June 26, 1974, a single pack of chewing gum became the first retail product sold with the help of a scanner in a Marsh supermarket in Troy, Ohio. Finally, all the billions of dollars invested and the decades of hard work had become a practical reality. Since then, the use of scanners has gradually increased. It is estimated that more than 60% of grocery stores now use scanners.

The technology used to print, scan, and program bar codes is today a $16-billion-a-year business. Unfortunately, Woodland himself never got rich from bar codes, although he was awarded the 1992 National Medal of Technology by President George Bush. The story of the bar code is a clear example of an idea ahead of time—a mismatch of opportunity and time.

No candy for alien

In 1981, Universal Studios contacted Mars and requested for permission to use their product M&M's in a new film they were making. The director's proposition was that he would use M&M's in the movie and the company in return would help promote the movie. This was a fairly common occurrence then and still is. Product placement deals provide extra income or promotion opportunities for filmmakers. However, the Mars brothers John and Forrest Mars, the owners of Mars Inc turned down the movie director's request. The film in question was *E.T. the Extra-Terrestrial*, directed and co-produced by Stephen Spielberg. The M&M's were needed for an important scene in the film in which Elliott, the little boy who befriended the alien E.T., uses candies to lure E.T. into his house. The Mars brothers felt that E.T. was so ugly that they refused their product to be used in the film. It was their belief that E.T. would frighten children. Following the refusal by Mars, Universal Studios approached another company called Hershey and cut a deal to use their new product called Reese's Pieces for the scene. The decision would prove to be one of the best business decisions ever made. E.T. turned out to be a big success. In 1983, E.T. surpassed 'Star Wars' as the highest grossing movie of all time. It remained in this position until 1993 when it was topped by 'Jurassic Park'. Overall, it grossed $792 million worldwide. From the partnership, Hershey witnessed a dramatic increase in the sales of Reese's pieces. Within two weeks of the release of E.T., Reese's sales tripled and continued to climb for months afterward. Jack Dowd, the then VP for new business development at Hershey summarised the whole encounter in these words, *"We didn't decide to put Reese's Pieces in it; Spielberg and his people did,"* he says. *"We were very lucky to get the **opportunity**; we were smart enough to take advantage of it, and professional enough to do it right."* (Emphasis mine)

The story of Reese's pieces success is a very good example of how time and opportunity can combine to create success. On the other hand, Mars' story is a good illustration of 'Missed Opportunity', another clear example of a mismatch of time and opportunity.

The crucial issue at this point is how can you take advantage of time and seize opportunities? Here are a few suggested steps to help you do this.

1. **Understand the drivers of every season**: Our world today is increasingly being driven by the desire for more convenience. There is an increased desire to do less and get more. Some people understand this driver and have made fortunes from providing services that meet this demand. Phones can now be used for many more things than they could be used for about 10 years ago, it's all about time and opportunity. The term 'user—friendliness' is increasingly becoming a 'money fetcher' in many areas of human existence. The more

user-friendly a thing is today, the more its demand. Again, it's all about time and opportunity—people plugging into the reigning culture of a season.

Convenience is not the only driver of this season; there are other drivers. Globally, there's an increasing demand for quality Customer Service. People want to get more value for their money. Businesses that continue to be successful understand this; hence the reason a lot of money is invested into staff training in the area of Customer Service. People don't mind paying more to be better served. As a matter of fact, people would happily pay more for the guarantee of being treated well. There was a time when customer service did not matter as much as it does now, it's all about time and opportunity. So for a minute, think about this—in your area of gifting or business, what are the important drivers at this point in time? When you identify the drivers, you will be able to identify opportunities that are inherent in the times.

2. **See beyond obstacles**: Many times, opportunity comes clouded by obstacles. Seldom is opportunity very obvious to everyone. The obstacles are the risks involved in going for the opportunity. Successful people focus more on the opportunity and not the

risks involved. No major success in life is achieved risk free. Some people would reckon that life itself is a risk. If we only focused on the risks in all of life, we would be severely handicapped. Imagine not taking the bus for fear of being involved in a road traffic accident or not flying for fear of a plane crash. Life would indeed be dull and boring. If you learn to focus on the positives however, life then suddenly becomes colourful. Wayne Dyer once stated, "When you change the way you look at things, the things you look at change as well." What is important is developing a strategy to mitigate or overcome the risk and reaching for the opportunity with both hands.

3. **Take care of the little things**: Opportunities don't always come big; many times it is a progression of successfully managing the little things. Where you are now is a preparation ground for where you want or need to be. You need to see every day and every position you find yourself in as an opportunity to get yourself prepared for where you want to be. By the time the big opportunity you want shows up, it is too late to prepare; you are either ready or not. I believe every person will get that one big opportunity that can potentially define the rest of their lives. This kind of opportunity does not give any notice, it just

happens. You would have had your whole life up to that point to prepare for it. Will you be ready?

"To every man there comes . . . that special moment when he is figuratively tapped on the shoulder and offered the chance to do a special thing unique to him and fitted to his talent. What a tragedy if that moment finds him unprepared or unqualified for the work which would be his finest hour" **Winston Churchill** (Emphasis mine)

There is often an inter-connection between opportunities. One opportunity leads to a bigger opportunity which in turn leads to another opportunity and the chain continues. For example, when a person takes up a job in an organisation even at the lowest cadre, that person has an opportunity to rise to the highest level in the same organisation. However the opportunity is likely to be presented in smaller forms of promotion through the ranks than a big leap to the very top. This is how most things happen in life, they start small and grow. Large leaps are the exception not the rule. This is perhaps the most important point a lot of people miss. Stop waiting for the big breakthrough; get busy now giving your best to each day where you are, in a matter of time, you will find yourself where you want to be. "If you can lay your head on your pillow each night knowing you gave 100% to your day, success will find you." Russell L. Mason

4. **Be willing to wait for the right time**

   It is one thing to see an opportunity; it is another thing to determine when the timing is right for taking the opportunity. Sometimes, opportunity may be perceived ahead of its time, as illustrated earlier in the story of the bar code. Success is determined in these instances by waiting for the right time.

   One of the best examples I know that illustrates this principle is the story of the Movie 'Avatar'. The director of the Movie, James Cameron wrote the first draft of the Movie in 1994. Filming however did not start until 2007 for the simple reason that the Movie director felt that he needed to wait for technology to catch up with his vision for the movie. Avatar eventually hit the cinema scenes in December, 2009. The result: Avatar broke several box office records including becoming the first film ever to gross over $2 billion worldwide. Clearly, the wait was worth it in every sense.

   You may be asking in your mind; what do I do if I'm not sure that the time is right for me to take an opportunity? The answer depends on why you feel the time may not be right. If it's because a very importance piece of the puzzle is missing as in the case of the Avatar film, then your best bet is to wait till you find that piece.

However, if it's just a question of not being sure whether or not the time is right, there are a few things you can do. Firstly, if possible, you may want to try out seizing the opportunity at a small level and see what the results are. This is what companies do when they survey the public opinion about a product or service. This exercise is bound to give you enough information to help guide your next decision.

Where trying out the opportunity on a small scale is improbable or impossible, you may want to consider seeking professional guidance or help from people who have experienced similar situations. Whatever you do, ensure that you go for the opportunity sooner or later. The only thing worse than an idea ahead of its time is an idea not acted upon. The worst outcome from going for an opportunity is failure to achieve your goal. However, in failure itself, lessons are learnt that could be helpful for future success.

CHAPTER 5

YOUR MOST DEPENDABLE ASSET: GOD

Perhaps you noticed that the discussion of the S.M.A.R.T acronym started with the second subject—Mind and not the first which is Source. This was deliberate on my part. I think the subject of Source (God) is the one asset that ties all the other assets together. This is the reason I have left it till the very end. Let me be quick to state that this chapter is not intended to be a religious discussion, but a discussion of my reality.

Accident or deliberate design?

World's famous author and leader, Dr Myles Munroe in his teaching titled 'The Power of purpose and Vision' opined that there are five questions that everyone wants to know the answer to. He calls them the five questions of the Human Heart. They are:

1. Who am I? This is the question of Identity.

2. Where am I from? This is the question of Source.

3. Why am I here? This is the question of Purpose.

4. What can I do? This is the question of Potential.

5. Where am I going to? This is the question of Destiny.

These five questions are inter-connected and an understanding of them is crucial to effective living. The question of Source is the subject of this chapter. This question is not about your Ethnicity, it's not even about your Ancestors, it goes back all the way to the very origin of man. This question is so crucial that over the years, a lot of effort has gone into trying to find an answer to this question.

There are two broad schools of thought about the origin of Man. These are popularly known as the Theory of Selection and the Theory of Creation. Most people subscribe to one or the other. The theory of Selection to summarise, postulates that Human life as it is today originated from a non-life form and has evolved over billions of years through many life forms into what is known today as the Human Being. The theory of creation which is grounded in many of the popular religions postulates that there is a Supreme Being popularly called God, who is omnipotent and eternal, who created Man and set in motion the process through which Man can continue to reproduce after himself.

I am not interested in discussing the various evidences for and against each of these theories, but to identify what is at the centre of each of these Belief Systems and the implications that they have on you as a person, depending on which School of thought you belong to. At the core of the selection theory is that Man and the world as a whole evolved by accident and from a non-life form. The creation theory has at its core that Man was a deliberate design of a Creator who had clear intentions about what he wanted to achieve.

By now, I guess you must have figured which of these Belief Systems I subscribe to. Yes you are right, I subscribe to the Creation theory. The reason is that for me to believe that somehow I am the product of an accident is to agree that there is no purpose to my life. It would mean for me that I was not born to do anything or become anyone. It would essentially mean that life is meaningless. Accidents and purpose don't go together. Purpose is always the product of deliberate intent and planning.

Secondly, when I look at the World as it is today, and I mean the natural world in this sense, I see order, I see structure. I see how the Lizard is an improvement over the fish and the monkey in turn an improvement over the Lizard. I see how the gravitational force was designed to keep the earth in its orbit. I see structure in nature; how one arm of nature depends on the other for its survival, without the other arm even being aware of the role it's playing in keeping the system together. Structure is never a product of accidents. To imagine that all these happened by accident is to assume that you can get a Volvo saloon out of a truck by dropping the truck in the middle of the motorway to be ramped into on all sides. You very well know that this is never going to happen. If you want a Volvo saloon, you create one.

The Importance of Source

Why is the question of Source so important? The understanding of a person's source is crucial for the following reasons:

1. **The Source determines the Purpose of a thing**
   In the natural, if you want to find out how anything functions and what it can be used for, you resort to the manufacturer's manual. The manufacturer's

manual is the guide from the source of that thing. The same is true for Man. Every person was born for a Purpose—to do something and become someone. That purpose was determined by Man's source—God. Unless and until that Purpose is discovered, a person cannot find fulfilment. This is why a person may be employed in a high paying job, have a lot of money and still not be fulfilled. The missing link is purpose. The person in question is not fulfilled because he/she has not connected with that which he/she was born to do.

If life was all about making a living, then the entire world system would be an absolute waste of space and time. Life is about making a difference. You have a unique part to play in doing this. Find it by connecting with your Source.

2. **The Source determines the value of a thing**

When an inventor has finished manufacturing his product, he/she places a price tag on it as a measure of the value of what the product is worth and how much it is to be exchanged for. No other person can determine the true value of product but the manufacturer. Similarly, the true value of Man can only be understood on the basis of what value the Source places on Man. It is written in the Good Book that the great teacher once said that, "What good is it for a man to gain the whole world, yet forfeit his soul? Or what can a man give in exchange for his soul?"

By saying this, he places the highest value possible on the human life. Put differently, Man is the most valuable resource on earth. That is how much you are worth. Even the whole world cannot be given in exchange for your life. I wish every person would know this truth. If everyone did, then no one would ever be able to make another person feel worthless. Stop defining your value by what other people may say about you or how the system of the world defines you. Your true value comes from your source.

3. **The Source determines the limits of possibilities of a thing**

If you do drive, the chances are that you have never driven to the maximum speed limit on the dashboard of your car, unless of course your car is a 'Formula One' car and you are a 'Formula One' driver. But if I were to ask you how fast you car drives, you are very likely to tell me the upper speed limit on your dashboard. Why? It's because the manufacturer says so. The implication is that the only person who can tell the limits of the possibilities of anything is the Source of that thing. Several times I have read of stories of people who had limits placed on what they could do or achieve by experts, but who went on to surpass all the limits. The explanation is clear, only the Source of Man can determine the limits of the possibilities of Man, every other person is at best guessing. What is the limit of Man's ability as defined by the Source? *". . . all things are possible to him who believes."* (Emphasis Mine)

History is full of stories of people who achieved feats that were reckoned as impossible in their times. Notable examples are the invention of the Aeroplane by the Wright Brothers, Man's travel into space and the design of the Automobile Car. All these examples are testaments to the limitless possibilities in every Man. Henry Ford once said, "I cannot discover that anyone knows enough to say definitely what is and what is not possible."

4. **The Source is essential to the survival of a thing.**
Although this point does not apply to most inanimate things, it certainly holds true for all animates including Man. Not only is the source of a thing responsible for bringing it to life, it is essential for maintaining

the very same life. There is an African adage which reads, "A River that forgets its source will run dry." The message in this adage holds equally true for Man as it does for the River.

In the account of Creation in the first chapter of Genesis, the first book in the Bible, God spoke to certain things to bring forth other things. For example, He spoke to the Waters to bring forth the fishes and other sea creatures. He also spoke to the land to bring forth plants and other animals. Here is the amazing bit; all of these creatures today depend on their source to survive. Fishes need water to survive, plants need the soil to survive and all animals directly or indirectly need the land to survive. If everything else needs its source to survive, it's plausible to conclude the same for Man.

It is been earlier established that God is the source of Man. Therefore, God is essential to Man's survival. He is your most dependable asset. The failure to recognise this is the reason for many of the struggles that people go through today, even in Developed Nations of the World. A lot of people feel what is most essential to their survival is a job or a Government. They fail to see the big picture that with or without a job or Government support, God is able to meet all of their needs. Here is a statement credited to the great teacher:

"So I tell you, don't worry about the things you need to live—what you will eat, drink, or wear. Life is more important than food, and the body is more important than what you put on it. Look at the birds. They don't plant, harvest, or save food in barns, but your heavenly Father feeds them. Don't you know you are **worth much more than they are***?*

You cannot add any time to your life by worrying about it. And why do you worry about clothes? Look at the wildflowers in the field. See how they grow. They don't work or make clothes for themselves. But I tell you that even Solomon, the great and rich king, was not dressed as beautifully as one of these flowers.

If God makes what grows in the field so beautiful, what do you think he will do for you? It's just grass—one day it's alive, and the next day someone throws it into a fire. But God cares enough to make it beautiful. Surely he will do much more for you. Your faith is so small!

Don't worry and say, 'What will we eat?' or 'What will we drink?' or 'What will we wear?'

That's what those people who don't know God are always thinking about. **Don't worry, because your Father in heaven knows that you need all these things**.

What you should want most is God's kingdom and doing what he wants you to do. Then he will give you all these other things you need. So don't worry about tomorrow. Each day has enough trouble of its own. Tomorrow will have its own worries." (Emphasis mine)

The message in this text is pretty clear. The Creator takes responsibility for all of his creations. All of God's creations have learnt to depend on God to meet their needs, all with the exception of Man. Cut out the worry, look to God to meet your needs; He is your most dependable asset.

The God-factor and the Mind

In the first chapter of this book, I established that your mind is your most expandable asset. It is the seat of all possibilities—all that a person can become is achieved at the level of the Mind. However, I also noted that the mind can be limited by self-imposed limits which often come from an individual's interpretation of reality. Reality unfortunately can be very subjective. Two people in the exact same situation can experience different realities. It is all a function of their individual thinking and what controls their thinking.

A person's quality of thinking is very crucial to who that person becomes. King Solomon states it succinctly, "Above all, be careful what you think, because your thoughts control your life." Your quality of thinking is a product of many things, two of the most important factors being your belief system and your level of awareness. These are in-turn fed by the quality of information that you expose yourself to. If you are constantly exposed to negative information, you are very likely to develop a negative belief system and be unaware of the possibilities inherent in you. Exposure to quality positive information produces the exact opposite effect.

As noted under the discussion of the Importance of the Source, your Source says you are limitless, only believe. God's manual, the Bible is full of lots of positive information that can be fed into your thought system to help you get a successful outcome in Life. This is God's desire for you, "I say this because I know the plans that I have for you." This message is from the LORD. "I have good plans for you. I don't plan to hurt you. I plan to give you hope and a good future."

The God-factor and People

The Community including every man's first community—The Family was God's idea not Man's. God's intent is that the family will be the first institution where an individual learns about obedience to law, responsibility to self and to the society at large. The family is supposed to be the unit that first sets up a person on the path to Success in life. The Wisest Man who ever lived once said, "Point your kids in the right direction— when they're old they won't be lost."

Unfortunately with the increasing breakdown of the family system, this role is lacking more and more. Recently, the Prince of Wales noted that Schools are not teaching valuable life skills to young people in Britain of today. In his own words,

> "Life skills, which consist of developing self esteem, self-confidence—looking people in the eye—all these things are not taught in schools or hardly at all . . . What it seems we're lacking is that element in educational process of character, character education alongside all the other bits and pieces which are of course important but, if at the end of the day you can't actually cope with the world

out there, the kind of interaction that's required of people, it is impossible it seems to me to manage, let alone to be employable."

I agree with Prince Charles. Schools need to do their bit in the training of young people to help them succeed in Life. However, the more I read his statement, the more I feel that the institution whose primary responsibility it is to help young people acquire essential social skills is the family. The failure of the family system is what makes today's society increasingly reliant on schools to fulfil this role. There is only so much that Schools can do. We must start re-building that Community spirit again. We must start teaching again strong social values that are family based. This is the way forward for a successful future as a Nation.

The God-factor and Money

The capacity to create wealth is a God-given ability innate in every person. This capacity was put there so you can activate it for wealth creation. The process for doing this has been discussed in great detail in the Chapters on Money and the Mind. When Wealth has been eventually created, what does

God intend that the Wealth be used for? I believe there are three basic things that Wealth should be used to achieve:

1. **To give you a good life**
   Life was not designed by God to be a struggle. As previously highlighted, God's plan for every person he created is for a good future. Money is one resource that can help a person enjoy the life that God has given. This is a good thing. There is so much more you can do with your life than whatever it is you are doing right now. Money is the one resource you can use to achieve this. Remember, it is your most deployable asset. You deserve the best that life can offer.

2. **To give your children leverage**
   Wouldn't it be nice to spare your children some of the hassles you went through to get to where you are today? Better still, wouldn't it be great to give them those opportunities you dreamed of but couldn't reach? I presume your answer to these questions is yes. This is one of God's purposes for money—to give your Children and generations after them a good life. King Solomon says, "It is good to have something to pass down to your grandchildren. But wealth hidden away by sinners will be given to those who live right."

3. **To make a difference in Society**
    Life is not all about you. God does not intend that your wealth will be all for yourself. Wealth is an opportunity to make a difference in the World. At the end of your life, you will not be remembered for how much wealth you possessed, but by what difference you made in people's lives. This is a noble and worthy cause. This is true Success.

The God-factor and Time

"He changes the times and seasons. He gives power to kings, and he takes their power away. He gives wisdom to people, so they become wise. He lets people learn things and become wise. He knows hidden secrets that are hard to understand. Light lives with him, so he knows what is in the dark and secret places." Daniel 2:21-22

God's hand is the invisible hand behind time. He sets time in place and determines the purpose for each season. He also determines the right time for each purpose. In the chapter on time, I emphasised the role of seasons and opportunities in achieving success. It was established that understanding a season and seizing the opportunity that comes with it is an important key for achieving success. You don't want to seize the opportunity ahead of the time; neither do you want to wait for the time to pass before you seize the opportunity. You want to get the timing right.

The text above taken from the biblical book of Daniel establishes that not only is God in control of time; He also knows and reveals those things that are hidden to man. So here's one more way that you can know when the right time to seize an opportunity is—follow God's guidance. Perhaps the most basic way through which God guides a person is through what is commonly called gut-feeling otherwise known as intuition. Your intuition can be a good but limited guide. Dr Wayne Dyer once established that, "If prayer is you talking to God, then intuition is God talking to you." Learn to follow your intuition.

To conclude this chapter, the best situation anyone can be, is in touch with their Source. It gives life purpose and meaning. It puts you in the best position to achieve Success. God is truly your most dependable asset.

CONCLUSION

You were born to succeed; success is intrinsic in your D.N.A. You have been equipped with the most essential assets to help you achieve success. It's time to look beyond your external circumstances and focus on the power within you and the people that are around you. Start approaching life with the right attitude, unleash the incredible power of your Mind and put your ideas to work. Be proactive in how you use your time; take full control of your life. Develop your relationships; people are your most invaluable asset. Above all, learn to depend on God for He is your source and will sustain you. Start living S.M.A.R.T. You will greatly succeed!

NOTES

Introduction

Blanden J, Steve Gibbons. The Persistence of poverty across generations: A view from two British Cohorts (Joseph Rowntree Foundation: Informing Change, April 2006).

CHAPTER 1

Joseph Keating, George Fleet. 'Thurman Fleet D.C. and the Early Years of the Concept-Therapy Institute'(A Presentation to the Association for the History of Chiropractic at the 17th Annual Conference on Chiropractic History, Texas Chiropractic College, February 23, 1997). Available from: http://www.chiro.org/Plus/History/Persons/ConceptTherapyInstitute/Fleet_Concept-Therapy_early-years.pdf[Accessed 22 October, 2012].

NOTES

Joseph C. Keating Jr, Chronology of Thurman G. Fleet, D.C. and the Concept Therapy Institute: Available from: http://www.chiro.org/Plus/History/Persons/ConceptTherapyInstitute/Fleet, T-chrono.pdf [Accessed 22 October, 2012].

Gary Schmid. Conscious vs Unconscious Information processing in the Mind-Brain. Available from: http://www.mind-body.info/files/conscious_vs_unconscious_thinking.pdf [Accessed 20 November, 2012].

Bruce Lipton. The Biology of Belief: Unleashing the Power of Consciousness, Matter & Miracles. March, 2011.

Damian Grammaticas. China cashes in on royal wedding. BBC News 24 January, 2011. Available from: http://www.bbc.co.uk/news/world-asia-pacific-12267108 [Accessed 25 January, 2011].

CHAPTER 2

Britain has highest divorce rate in EU. Mail Online. Available from: http://www.dailymail.co.uk/news/article-52829/Britain-highest-divorce-rate-EU.html [Accessed 23 February, 2013].

Jack Doyle. Under 18s commit a quarter of all crimes: Young offenders responsible for more than a million crimes in just one year. Available from: http://www.dailymail.co.uk/

news/article-2150187/Under-18s-commit-quarter-crimes-Young-offenders-responsible-million-crimes-just-year.html [Accessed 23 February, 2013].

'In Developing Countries nearly 500,000 women die from complications of pregnancy and childbirth every year'. The World Bank 14 June 2010. Available from: http://data.worldbank.org/news/500000-women-die-from-pregnancy-complications [Accessed 23 March 2012].

CHAPTER 3

Ecclesiastes 10:19b. The Holy Bible (Easy-to-Read Version).

Robert Kiyosaki, Sharon Lechter. Rich Dad, Poor Dad: What the Rich teach their Kids about Money that the Poor and Middle Class do not! April, 2001.

Cohort Estimates of Life Expectancy at age 65. UK Department of Works and Pension, April, 2011. Available from: http://statistics.dwp.gov.uk/asd/asd1/adhoc_analysis/2011/life_expectancy.pdf [Accessed 23 July 2012]

Long term State Pension sustainability: increasing the State Pension age to 67. UK Department of Works and Pension, December 2011. Available from: http://www.dwp.gov.uk/

docs/state-pension-age-67-impact-assessment.pdf [Accessed 23 July 2012]

Genesis 41: 33-36, 56-57.

Benjamin Carson, Cecil Murphey. Gifted Hands: The Ben Carson Story. January, 1992.

Carson Scholars Fund, General Information about Dr. Benjamin Carson. Available from: http://carsonscholars.org/dr-ben-carson/general-information [Accessed 27 July, 2012]

Mortgage Overpayment Calculator, HBSC UK. Available from: https://mortgages.hsbc.co.uk/overpayment-calculator [Accessed 27 July, 2012]

Alice Philipson, Lucy Kinder. Wimbledon 2012: Andy Murray could earn £100m if he wins in final. The Telegraph, 08 July, 2012. Available from: http://www.telegraph.co.uk/sport/tennis/wimbledon/9385189/Wimbledon-2012-Andy-Murray-could-earn-100m-if-he-wins-in-final.html [Accessed 20 September, 2012]

Student Loan Repayment Calculator—The Complete University Guide. Available from: http://www.thecompleteuniversityguide.co.uk/student-loan-repayment-calculator [Accessed 20 September, 2012]

CHAPTER 4

Ecclesiastes 9:11. The Holy Bible (Complete Jewish Bible Version).

Charles Fishman. The Killer App—Bar None. American Way, 1 August 2001 Issue. Available from: http://hub.aa.com/en/aw/so-woodland-bar-code-bernard-silver-drexel-university [Accessed 24 Aug 2011]

Tony Seideman. Barcodes Sweep the World. Available from: http://www.barcoding.com/information/barcode_history.shtml [Accessed 21 January 2013]

David Van Biema. Life is Sweet for Jack Dowd as Spielberg's Hit Film E.T. has Film Lovers Picking up the (Reese's) Pieces. Archive Vol 18. No. 4; 26 July, 1982.

Alexander Marquardt. Did Avatar Borrow from Soviet Sci-Fi Novels? ABC News, 14 January, 2010. Available from: http://abcnews.go.com/Entertainment/avatars-james-cameron-borrow-soviet-sci-fi-novels/story?id=9561339 [Accessed 21 January 2013]

Esme Deprez. 'Avatar' Tops Box Office, Passes $2 Billion Worldwide (Update 1). Business Week, 31 January, 2010.

Available from: http://www.webcitation.org/5pBiriyeR [Accessed 21 January 2013]

CHAPTER 5

Mark 8:36. The Holy Bible (Modern King James Version).
Mark 9:23. The Holy Bible (Modern King James Version).
Matthew 6:25-34. The Holy Bible (Easy-to-Read Version).
Proverbs 4:23. The Holy Bible (Easy-to-Read Version).
Jeremiah 29:11. The Holy Bible (Easy-to-Read Version).
Proverbs 22:6. The Holy Bible (The Message Version).

Hayley Dixon. Schools are failing to teach life skills and leaving youth unemployable, Prince Charles warns. The Telegraph, 30 January, 2013. Available from: http://www.telegraph.co.uk/news/uknews/prince-charles/9836204/Schools-are-failing-to-teach-life-skills-and-leaving-youth-unemployable-Prince-Charles-warns.html [Accessed 01 February, 2013]

Proverbs 13:22. The Holy Bible (Easy-to-Read Version).